Toddler Swimming

Thank you!

A special word of thanks goes to my personal editor Mr. Gottfried Ahrendt, the photographer Ms. Mathilde Kohl, and the numerous parents and children who so willingly took part in the photo sessions.

Dr. Lilli Ahrendt

Note:

In my first book, **Baby Swimming**, I deal with the development of a child in his first year of life, and the promotion of movement appropriate to this development. In this book, however, I look at child development and the methodical and didactic factors of swimming with 1-year-olds (young toddlers) and 2- year-olds (toddlers) together, seeing as there is no definite dividing line between these two age groups.

General comment:

In this book, the term "parent" also applies to any other accompanying person who is important to the toddler.

The book has been written in the masculine form for reader-friendly reasons only. The feminine form is implied to the same extent where appropriate.

Lilli Ahrendt

TODDLER SWIMMING

THE FUNDAMENTS OF CHILD DEVELOPMENT AND GUIDANCE THROUGH PARENT-CHILD SWIMMING DURING THE 2ND AN 3RD YEARS OF LIFE

With Photos by Mathilde Kohl

MEYER
& MEYER
SPORT

Original Title: Kleinkindschwimmen
© 2002 by Meyer & Meyer Verlag, Aachen
Translation: Anne Lammert

Editor of the German Series: Prof. Kurt Wilke

British Library Cataloguing in Publication Data
A catalogue record for this book is available from the British Library

Lilli Ahrendt:
Toddler Swimming
Oxford: Meyer & Meyer Sport (UK) Ltd., 2005
ISBN 1-84126-164-5

© 2005 by Meyer & Meyer Sport (UK) Ltd.
Aachen, Adelaide, Auckland, Budapest, Graz, Johannesburg, New York,
Olten (CH), Oxford, Singapore, Toronto
Member of the World
Sports Publishers' Association (WSPA)
www.w-s-p-a.org

Printed and bound in Germany by: TZ Verlag
by: ISBN 1-84126-164-5
E-Mail: verlag@m-m-sports.com

Contents

Editor's Foreword 7

I   INTRODUCTION 8

II   FUNDAMENTS OF CHILD DEVELOPMENT AND
     TODDLER SWIMMING 12
1   Water 13
     1.1 An Everyday Element 15
     1.2 An Element of Play 16
     1.3 An Element of Danger: Teaching Safety 17

2   The Toddler—Second and Third Years of Life 22
     2.1 Physical and Motor Development—from Initial Independent
         Steps to a Varied Repertoire of Movements 23
     2.2 Sense Organs and Perception—Increase in Stimulus
         Processing and World Discovery Using Eyes and Hands 31
     2.3 Relationship and Speech Behavior—
         from Autonomy Up to the Strive for Independence 35
     2.4 Playing and Learning Behavior—from Imitating and
         Performing to Trying Things Out Oneself 37
     2.5 Hygienic Behavior—Growing Away from a Diaper 40
     2.6 Noticeable Movement Defects and Disturbances in Perception . . .43

3   Parents and Course Instructors .48
     3.1 The Parental Role in the Process of a Child's Personality
         Development 49
     3.2 The Course Instructor as an Advisor, a Creative Designer,
         and the Person to Whom Toddler and Parent Relate 53

4   Toddler Swimming 56
     4.1 The Meaning Behind and Objectives of Movement,
         Play and Sport for Toddlers 57
     4.2 The Concept of Interactive Movement Stimulation—
         Exploring the Water World Together 61
     4.3 Learning of Movement and Swimming Behavior 62
     4.4 Research Findings, Success Anticipated, and the End Results:
         And When Does a Child Finally Learn to Swim? 67

Toddler Swimming

III THE PRACTICAL SIDE OF TODDLER SWIMMING 70

5 The Planning and Organization of a Course 71
5.1 Planning and Carrying Out a Course 71
5.2 Information for Parents and Game Suggestions for
Showering and Bathing at Home .73
5.3 Some Points of Advice for the Swimming Pool 77
5.4 Hygiene and the Prevention of Illness 78
5.5 First Aid, the Duties of Care and Responsibility to a Child 81

6 Course Contents and Practice 88
6.1 Run of Events and Contents of Course 89
6.2 Constructing a Lesson, Lesson Content, and Creative
Structure of a Lesson 93
6.2.1 Basic Movement Forms and Basic Skills in Water . . .103
6.2.2 Gymnastic Exercises and Climbing About on a
Parent in the Water 107
6.2.3 Grip Techniques with Ideas for Games and Exercises . .111
6.2.4 Getting Accustomed to Water and Diving Techniques . . .133
6.2.5 Ideas for Movement Using a "Training Circuit" 141
6.2.6 Perception Exercises 147
6.2.6.1 Optical Area 147
6.2.6.2 Acoustic Area 148
6.2.6.3 Tactile Area 150
6.2.6.4 Body Orientation 151
6.2.6.5 Spatial and Positional Orientation 152
6.2.6.6 Reaction Training 153
6.2.7 Playing with Materials and in a Group 155
6.2.8 Rituals and Songs 163
6.2.9 Ways of Relaxing in the Water 168
6.3 Swimming and Buoyancy Aids .173

IV APPENDIX 180
7 Alphabetical Index 181
8 Photo & Illustration Credits 183

Editor's Foreword

Although a child in his second and third year of life masters the majority of his world on dry land, the scope of movement offered by water is ideal for this age group, too.

As opposed to a baby's movements, a toddler's movements are controlled to a large extent by his own free will. Water, a pliable liquid element with buoyant force, offers a child unique methods of perception and control in his curious conquest of his environment, as long as he is faced with pleasant, fear-free, playful situations.

Water, and the feeling of one's body in water, then become an exciting adventure, encouraging deliberate effective behavior, binding parent and child through mutual experience, and paving the way towards confident, life-saving swimming abilities.

Above all, Lilli Ahrendt centers her work around the advancement and guidance of a child's development. Toddler development is thus the central theme in this book, as well as being the starting point for her methodical guidance of parents, course instructors, and all those involved with toddler swimming, whether on the planning, organizational or practical side.

In addition to pedagogical development, the author does not neglect to inform in practical detail about gripping and securing a small child's body in the water, and to offer advice on factors which might seem trivial, but are, nevertheless, important for the success of the course, such as temperature, hygiene, materials or swimwear.

Even with all these technical details, Lilli Ahrendt goes to show that toddler swimming is not a mere instruction of movement techniques, but rather is based on trusting and sensitive interaction in the water between parent and child.

Cologne, November 2004   *Kurt Wilke*

I INTRODUCTION

This book is the sequel to the book **Baby Swimming**. Whereas baby swimming concentrated on parent-child swimming in the first year of a child's life, this book deals with *toddlers,* and therefore, also the development phases and methods of encouraging this development through parent-child swimming in the second and third years of life.

The term *swimming* for this age group refers to a child's oriented movement in water, supported by parents or buoyancy aids, as well as his independent desire to move within water. Swimming on his own[1] is a skill which a child can learn from the age of four, at the earliest. Apart from a child's mental maturity and motivation, this particularly depends on the growth of the limbs, as well as the related force-load relationship and the child's motor-coordinative skills.

As with little kids doing gymnastics, it goes without saying that the basic elements of movement in water with parental support must be tried out and tested under the course instructor's expert guidance. Water itself is an exceptional medium, and offers a suitable scope for playing and frollicking about.

The first steps toward learning swimming are set methodically according to age. The first hurdle is getting accustomed to the water, and coping with it. This is initiated within the framework of parent-child swimming, both integrally and interactively, i.e. the children are left to discover the pleasure of movement together with their parents, gradually and without any pressure of performance. They then experience this by moving around, jumping, dipping and diving, as well as with various games, gymnastic and relaxation exercises. Swimming can be carried out in one's leisure time as a *sport with perspective,* throughout one's whole life, and in all generations as a common family sport.

---

1 *Swimming* here refers to locomotion in deep water over a distance of 12 meters (*Penguin badge*), or 25 meters (*Seahorse badge*) with certain jumping and diving skills. These early swimming badges certify a child's first swimming achievements, carried out under supervision.

Successful toddler swimming calls for qualified instruction under suitable conditions in warm water (about 32° celsius) with the parents being able to stand up in the water. The groups should be divided up according to age and experience since a child's movement repertoire expands rapidly in the first few years.

The lesson is to be directed toward playfully enhancing movement in water in combitantion with pedagogical supervision, characterizing the intended and deliberate actions of both the course instructor, and the parents with their child.

It is possible to start parent-child swimming at any time. Those phases typical for the second year of life, e.g. *fear of being separated from his parents* (at about 13 months), *phase of defiance* (about 18 months), *fear of deep water* (about 24 months) or even the general orientation problems in unfamiliar sitiations or places (*fear of new experiences*) may affect the lesson at certain stages.

Toddler swimming consciously intensifies the parent-child relationship. What was once a waving and kicking baby becomes a clinging toddler or even a rebellious fighter wishing to get his own way; a child who has a completely different opinion than his parents in the water is suddenly afraid or no longer wants to be held up although he is not able to swim.

It is important to accept these stages of development as mere phases, and to patiently get through them with compromises.

Being able to play and splash around with his parents in the water is an activity which a child enjoys. Waves and splashes are a method of getting him used to the water which are fun for him, and are not something he is afraid of; jumping into the water and diving under become one of his favorite games as he is held in the familiar protective arms of his parents.

The lessons are designed to be integral in content, promoting mental, motor, social and emotional skills to an equal extent. Creative lesson structure enables the parents and children to experience a variety of movements with sheer pleasure.

Toddler swimming can lay strong foundations for gaining confidence in the water, a healthy process which—for a child's own interest in health and sport—can be continued later with swimming. In general, a child can only consciously learn proper swimming technique from the age of three at the earliest, as he then has the necessary maturity in cognitive, physical and motor skills.

Parents who hinder their child from playing and experimenting in the water at an early age, who somewhat heteronomously allow a child into the water when fully equipped with buoyancy aids, and permanently warn him of the dangers involved instead of accompanying him and encouraging him to get familiar with this medium, run the risk of causing their child to have a phobia of water. This in turn may result in future swimming lessons being long, tedious, difficult, and anything but relaxing.

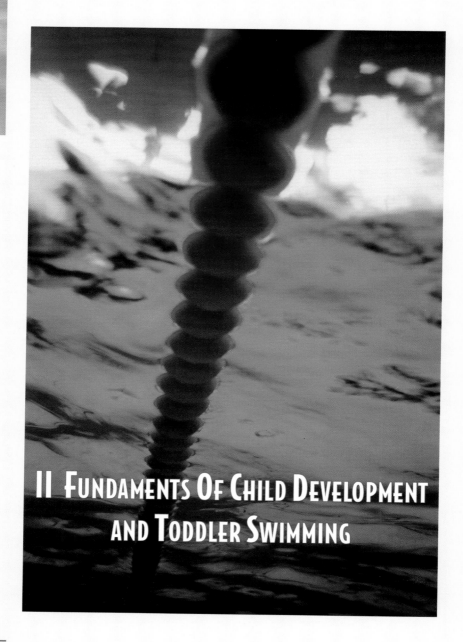

II FUNDAMENTS OF CHILD DEVELOPMENT AND TODDLER SWIMMING

1 Water

Water, an element of movement in its own endless cycle, has a fascinating attraction on us. This is particularly visible in certain situations when people are drawn towards the beach, or to a roaring mountain lake. Even in our day-to-day life we love a shower; in the same way, we also feel reborn after swimming.

For a child in a discovery phase, water is a creative and exciting area of adventure and experience. Water binds together by enclosing both child and parent, allowing them to act and react very close to one another. Its distinctive permeable characteristic means that a child must be continuously supervised and supported. A child needs this assistance due to his inability to swim.

A child's fundamental mental attitudes are shaped in the first few years of life in particular. If a child is offered a playful encounter with water during this time, and a good relationship develops between himself and the water, he will continue to retain this positive attitude to water in later years.

Water does not only symbolically seize us in its entirety, but physically and mentally, too. Being able to cope with water, and hold one's own in the water gives a child psychological strength. Such experiences boost his self-confidence, courage and enthusiasm, which he can then pass on to his day-to-day situations. Movement in water has also been a recognized and valued method of personality advancement for a long time now.

1.1 An Everyday Element

Water is not just there for drinking; it's also necessary for our daily body hygiene. From the second year of life onwards, a child can already take a bath by himself, i.e. not just together with his parents, when the water is no higher than 30cm, and an anti-sliding mat is on the tub bottom. Toys, such as sponges or beakers of various sizes encourage the child to stay seated for a little longer while all the time playfully discovering water.

In order to work on their body scheme, it helps when children learn in a playful manner how to wash different parts of their body with a wash-cloth. An older brother or sister, or a doll can bathe at the same time, so as to give a good example, too. A quick shower before a diaper change can also be introduced.

Washing hair at this age proves to be trickier. As the children are still a bit unsteady in regards to keeping their balance, they are not able to stay in upright position, and lean their head backwards.

For the same reason, the supine position is also generally unfavourable for this procedure. It is better when the child is able to hold on to something in either sitting or standing position, and to close his eyes. His parents should use a mild children's shampoo and rinse it out again quickly with the shower jet.

1.2   An Element of Play

Water is a particularly exciting element for toddlers. Here they can make their first experiments in physics, i.e. buoyancy, resistance, pressure and temperature. They also get to know the three-dimensional possibilities of moving their limbs. They use water on the beach as a binder for building castles and ditches. In the bath, they use foam to wallpaper the tiles and wet feet leave footprints.

The consistency of water makes it possible to put it in one's mouth and spit it out again, to blow in it and blubber, to spoon it up and pour it out, to dribble and sprinkle, to watch it flowing, and observe it on our skin. A child satisfies his curiosity with these experiences, and is challenged to continue with his creativity.

1.3 An Element of Danger: Teaching Safety

A well meant word of warning should make all readers aware of just how vital it is for small children to learn the skills of swimming for their own protection, particularly when we harmlessly encounter water in every day-to-day situation, such as when brushing our teeth, bathing ourselves, walking alongside a river, leisure time at a lake, observing pond activities etc.

All people who are involved with children should be alarmed when e.g. The German Federal Office For Statistics (VIII A1 Health 1999) reports that the number of deaths caused by drowning alone among children of 1-5 years of age (58 in total) was almost twice as high as for children of 5-10 years of age, and almost 15 times higher than for babies (< 1 year). The statistics of the German Life Saving Association for all of Germany in the first six months of 2001[2] showed 181 cases of drowning, 10% of which (18) involved children under the age of five.

Most accidents occur in natural waterways or there is no further explanation for the accident. In comparison, accidents in the bath tub or the swimming pool make up a minor part of the total accidents. Nevertheless, it is clear from the statistics that a toddler as a non-swimmer represents a target group that is in serious danger, both due to his strong urge to move around and explore, as well as his lack of experience. His physical abilities are also a considerable hindrance to rescuing himself.

---

2   Personal advance information, official publication in 2002

It is important for parents to be sensitive to the dangers in and around water, and to learn to estimate their child's abilities. In a questionnaire of parents with and without regular participation in toddler swimming courses, it became clear that parents with course experience indicated better safety behavior toward their child when on vacation.

Thus, toddler swimming is a form of safety training through education along with the parents' practical hands-on experience with their child in water. Dangers can be estimated more realistically when parents have real practice in tackling the situation, and with the help of playful training of certain rules of behavior, the course instructor can educate both children and parents in a true-to-life manner.

A spontaneous experiment brought a further aspect to light—the parents' own experience with water.

In baby and toddler courses, they are given instructions on how to look after their child in a proper, expert way. Many parents gain access to water again through their children, and with regular course visits they strengthen their belief in their own personal skills; they learn to be confident with their child.

These experiences ensure a more realistic assessment of real-life occurrences, even outside the course, and are useful for both children *and* parents in mastering leisure and vacation situations. It is, after all, the parents who hold their child and watch over him in the water, and in the case of an emergency, should be able to save him.

As long as a child is unable to swim, he requires constant supervision. Overprotective parents, with endless warnings of the dangers lurking, hinder the child from making his own experiences with water and learning how to protect himself. I would like to point out here that persistent use of swimming aids (e.g. wings) does not guarantee the child's safety, no matter how near one is.

Accidents which occur as a result of slipping in the bath can be prevented with an anti-slip mat on the floor of the bath. The baby should never be left alone while bathing. For this reason towels and other necessary utensils should be laid in place beforehand.

In regard to swimming pools, ponds, or rainwater tanks, all of which could be a potential threat to a child's life, private pool owners are even legally obligated to take safety precautions in the form of fences, pool covers, or protective railings when the basin is not supervised.

Recommendations for safety training:

◆ A child may only enter changing rooms and showering facilities accompanied by their guardian/ "trust person."
◆ If the child is already able to walk, he should—even without going hand-in-hand—learn to find the *meeting place* by himself, e.g. the warm bench where the familiar swim bag has been placed, and then wait there. This can be a set task from time to time; parents should observe their child's behavior in hiding.
◆ If a parent has to go to the toilet, or the changing rooms during the lesson, he must take his child with him, or leave him exclusively *under the supervision* of a person present.
◆ When killing time, e.g before a lesson, the child should be entertained with his own toys outside the pool area. If it is already possible to enter the pool, parents must always accompany their child into the water.
◆ Parent and child either enter the water together, or else the child after the parent. The children all jump into the water after a specific signal.
◆ Throughout the lesson, one must ensure that the child does actually follow orders for a short time, e.g. "Hold onto the edge, I'll be with you now" or "Stay seated, I'll go and get the ball" in order to be sure that one can depend on the child when the parent moves away for a moment.
Parents and children should strengthen their relationship of trust here, too. Promised word and action convey safety.
◆ After swimming, parents and children leave the pool, shower area and changing rooms together.
For practical purposes, parents can also head out of the shower into the changing room, and ask the child to follow him soon after, provided, of course, that the supervision by another parent has been arranged beforehand.

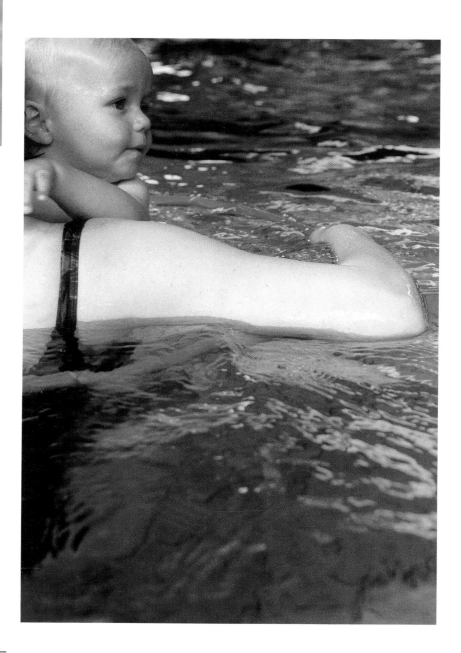

Other swimming rules:

◆ A toddler should take part in a swimming lesson when he is physically fit and free of infectious illnesses.

◆ One should stay in warm water (approx. 32°) for no longer than 45 minutes. If the child appears to be freezing at any time one must leave the water immediately.

◆ A child should only dive down when it has already learned the protective reaction, i.e. to avoid the danger of swallowing water, of water going down the wrong way, or of breathing in water. When the child has learned this technique, he will generally be well-prepared, stressfree and attentive.

◆ One ought to be wary about the occasionally propagated method of self-rescue[3], whereby the child has either to remain in supine position in the water for a certain amount of time without being held, or is dropped into the water.
There is a danger here of water intoxication. It is disapproved of for pedagogical and psychological reasons as the child is regularly subjected to an unjustified mental and physical stress situation, the possible consequence of this being a fear of water.
Such a method will certainly not enhance a child's motivation to want to be able to swim. Contrary to the integral method of teaching, this method is actually abusing the child's trust and confidence in his parents' protective abilities.

An optimal run of events is when the child can detach himself step by step from the safe and familiar parental care, and is able to rely on his own abilities. He should get to cross the "Just-about-made-it" boundary, and experience the enjoyment of growing in independence.

---

3   Babies and toddlers are drilled to turn into supine position after falling into the water, and to hold this position despite having swallowed water.

2 The Toddler– Second and Third Years of Life

2.1 Physical and Motor Development–From Initial Independent Steps to a Varied Repertoire of Movements

A toddler's physical proportions and appearance are similar to those of a baby. His head accounts for about a quarter of the total body length, his arms and legs are short in relation to his body. The body's center of gravity starts changing from the fourth year of life onwards when his limbs grow significantly. His balancing abilities improve, and his swimming movements become more effective. In the first two years of life, a child's knees are always slightly bent; the legs are in a slight bandy-legged position. The characteristic head proportions are a large cerebral skull, and a small facial skull, the cheeks are full, the eye section large. Lumbar lordosis develops in the spinal column due to the toddler's ability to stand upright and the increased walking movements; the pelvis tilts forward, which also explains why the abdomen bulges out to the front. As the skeletal system is still very soft, and the plantar arch can only develop as a result of walking, slight malformations can appear. Walking barefoot, wearing light clothes, and having variety in movement all help to counteract this problem.

A fast weight increase and large growth in length are the typical features of a toddler's physical development. However, these vary considerably depending on hereditary factors, the child's development, nutrition, and sex. A one-year-old child has generally tripled his birth weight (to approx. 12 kg) and has grown in length by about 50% to approximately 75cm. His breathing rate and heartbeat, on the other hand, are slightly lower than that of a baby. The breathing rate is approximately 35 breaths per minute. The flat diaphragm breathing typical for a baby is replaced by the deeper thorax breathing method. The pulse rate—the shock wave transferred from the heart to the arteries—is around 100 beats per minute in the second year of life. Blood pressure—the pressure of flowing blood in the vascular system produced by the strength of the heart muscles—goes up from 60/35 mm Hg in the first year of life to 80/50 mm hg in the second year.[4] Due to the heart's high performance capacity, physical overtaxing hardly ever occurs. A toddler can regenerate effectively with short breaks.

---

4   For comparison: An adult's blood pressure is about 120/80 mm Hg.

Immunological maturity of function occurs in the first 2-3 years of life. Teething, greater oral contact with surrounding materials and more frequent contact with other children of the same age all go to make toddlers vulnerable to infections. Infections which have been actively coped with help to build up the child's immune system.

The recommended vaccinations (measles, mumps, rubella, diphtheria-pertussis-tetanus, Haemophilus influenzae and polymyelitis) offer protection from dangerous diseases; a doctor will give booster injections from 15 months onwards.

The toddler rapidly continues developing his motor skills. A baby under one year has had to fight against gravity in order to pull himself up and has learned how to sit, stand, and move around objects. In his second year of life, he spends most of his time trying out free standing, walking and crouching; his own eagerness to climb encourages him to negotiate the next floor level, e.g. on the stairs. His urge to remain in upright position is remarkable; changing diapers when he is lying down is hardly possible anymore.

His ability to keep his balance when standing and walking is still somewhat instable. He wobbles and falls a lot; his walking pattern is broad and staggered (duck walk); he balances by holding his arms out to the side.

By intensively tackling his world of objects and social environment, the child works out a varied repertoire of movement as the year goes on:

- He learns to walk, fall and get up again, even on uneven surfaces.
- He walks backwards, balances, learns to climb up and down.
- He trudges along although still lacking in coordination, changes direction, tempo and rhythm of movement while doing so.
- He climbs stairs one step at a time holding onto the rail, first upwards and then downwards at a later stage.
- He copes with his body weight, e.g. hanging on a pole or pushing up on his hands.
- He frequently plays in crouched position and practices keeping his balance while doing so.
- He eats simple things with a spoon (second year), and later with a special children's knife and fork, (third year) thus improving his ability to make slow, concentrated movements, and to carry out a movement accurately.
- He wants to become more and more involved in household activities; he makes his first attempts at dressing himself, thus working on self-teaching skills.

The child develops an incredible movement urge. He is enthusiastic when he

- discovers sounds, rhythms and movements, such as rocking and swinging by himself.
- can test his holding and stretching skills, and see how his body works.
- can bounce up and down in somebody's hands, jump off a platform, and later jump over obstacles by himself (high and far).
- can wallow and roll around, slide and creep through tunnels
- can carry objects, pull, push, roll, kick and throw things (one-handed straight shot, double-handed under-handed throw, throwing to somebody, and at a target) and catch them. Through this he learns how to

measure his dosage of strength effort against resistance, and test his strength effort on objects. He also tests his spatial orientation, coordination, reaction and skillfulness; he learns how to adapt to situations, and follow mobile objects with his eyes, and estimate their speed.

◆ is allowed to test his strength by climbing and clambering.

From the age of two, his willpower to carry out independent actions grows. He often overestimates his abilities as he discovers many new and difficult movements: he is constantly improving his skills, and soon tries to stand on one leg, works on his handedness[5], and already throws with a better aim, he draws holding the crayon in a "paw-grip," and carries out activities with both hands, e.g. building bricks.

Development really charges ahead when he starts climbing stairs with alternate steps, or when he tries his luck on the tricycle by pedalling alternately.

A child in his third year of life balances on the wall, and can stand on one leg for about one second, much to the alarm of his grandparents. His fine motor skills become more controlled, e.g. when lifting up a full cup, or when trying to catch a ball with both hands.

As every movement process seems to be relatively new for a toddler, he constantly feels encouraged to imitate everything.

Thus, he also tries to clap and sing along with familiar songs. His fine motor actions may still be relatively inaccurate while gross motor activities get steadier and more targeted all the time.

---

[5] Handedness refers to the preference for a particular side.

A toddler appears to possess endless amounts of motor energy. At the beginning of his second year of life, he still needs a supportive hand for walking, by the end of this year, his radius of motor and social action has expanded considerably: he almost playfully runs away to actively and impetuously explore his environment; a process which calls on the parents to decide between independence, and protective action, i.e. what they think he is capable of managing, and how/whether they should protect him.

The development of basic motor skills during the second and third years of life:

Walking
◆ From about one year onwards (10-18 months)

Running
◆ From approx. two-and-a-half, initially with his arms out wide to help him keep his balance.
◆ His stride gradually gets longer and faster; he starts to bend his arms more often.

Climbing
◆ A child can climb up a play ladder from about the age of one to one-and-a-half; the downwards climb comes a little later.
◆ At the same age and with some help, he also climbs over little obstacles (pathway, benches).
◆ At the age of two-and-a-half, he can go up and down steps, and is well able to climb over obstacles.

Jumping
◆ From the age of two, toddlers begin to hop down from a small height, or jump over lines, sticks or ropes; both feet set down together (similar to a frog-leap).

Throwing

◆ He starts off practicing different throws: straight shot (baseball throw) i.e. overhand, and the underhand throw (ten-pin bowling).[6]

Catching

◆ This begins at the age of 20 months; the toddler stretches his arms out parallel in front of him, but is not able to coordinate pulling them in again towards his body. These are skills which he does not learn until his third year of life.

The characteristics of the movement process in the second year of life are as follows:

◆ little strength of movement.
◆ slow movement performance, not quick in reaction.
◆ narrow and relatively small spatial volume.
◆ short swings of his arms and legs.
◆ movements are not rhythmical.
◆ actions are still quite jerky and clumsy (not elastic or fluent).
◆ limb movements are not yet in combination with the trunk; difficulties keeping balance.
◆ idle stride movements when running, jumping, hopping and throwing. The movements are not yet constant and economical.

The reasons can be explained by

◆ the muscles, as they are still in the developmental process.
◆ the distribution of muscular strength (force-load relationship is not yet in balance due to the misbalanced body proportions)
◆ the lack of coordinative skills, as these are only beginning to develop, as well as reaction duration (no quick reactions, it takes *ages and ages*).
◆ the toddler's totally *carefulness* of movement, a sign that he is in the *trying out phase*.
◆ motor practice, which is still trailing behind the stimulative process in the *learning phase*. From a brain physiology view of things, a dynamic motor stereotype must be formed beforehand.

Movements are carried out more consciously, accurately and steadily in a child's third year of life thanks to imitation and variation.

An average child in the second and third year of life has developed as follows:

1.Endurance:

The child shows endurance when playing. He is already able to concentrate well. By frequently changing playing activities with varying load, central nervous fatigue is postponed, and local fatigue is not possible. The activities themselves do not yet go on for long; short but fast-changing performances at low intensity takes place. These are possible due to the as yet underdeveloped cardio-pulmonary system (high pulse and breathing rate at rest).

2. Coordinative skills:

Toddlers stick to the area of gross coordination. Motor abilities, such as orientating oneself, making contact, adapting to situations, differentiating, and keeping balance seem to stagnate even if toddlers do like to try balancing.

3. Flexibility:

This is a curious development among toddlers. Whereas the bigger joints have good bending abilities, stretching is a skill which has not developed yet.

4. Speed:

It is not yet possible to talk about performance here as a child in these two years increases his movement repertoire first with nearly every action he does; this is accompanied by many first-time acts.

---

6   In the first year of life, one can more often observe the preliminary form of the straight shot, something similar to dropping the ball when the child takes down all objects he can reach.

2.2   Sense Organs and Perception–Increase in Stimulus Processing and World Discovery Using Eyes and Hands

In the first year of a child's life, his sensory organs are maturing all the time, and brain physiological and intellectual classification (*sensory motor integration*) begins. In his first few months, a baby initially perceives touch only, but is not able to consciously classify and localize them; a toddler, however, selects and integrates his impressions in a considerably more detailed and differentiated form. He directs his attention more clearly at things and carries out his movements much more deliberately. He does not learn to control his feelings better until after his third year of life. A toddler develops a picture of his body's existence, its limits and movement abilities, and with increasing self-discovery and lingual expressive abilities, continues to build up his body scheme in his third year of life through his kinesthetic perception. His balance reactions (feeling for position and movement, postural reflexes) and his position-room orientation improve considerably.

At the beginning, a baby recognizes contrasts only. There is a dramatic improvement in a toddler's visual acuity; by the age of two, his eyesight will have already reached 50% of that of an adult. While a baby discovers objects primarily with his mouth (*oral touching*), a one-year-old child, thanks to his manual skillfulness, explores more and more objects through intensive examination (*visual exploration*). By the end of his second year, his sense of touch is not as dominant anymore; his mouth is no longer the most important tactile organ. At the age of three he can differentiate in colors, both visually and lingually. He cannot master spatial vision before the age of four; he then can estimate short distances.

A toddler deciphers *object permanency* i.e. he consciously registers the existence or removal of an object. A child between one and one-and-a-half finds objects that he himself had thrown away or hidden. He is aware of connections: small building bricks are placed into bigger containers, sounds are identified and where they come from, he points to his and other persons' parts of the body. A two-year-old can already take in shapes and colors; this is evident in allocation games. As he becomes more and more aware of his own body, he can already differentiate between male and female at the age of two to two-and-a-half. At the age of three, depending on his language development, he is generally able to say parts of his body, and can identify different sizes. The term two as an amount is a detail which he can comprehend.

In regards to acoustic stimulus the child can distinguish between vocal signals of emotion; he likes producing his own sounds and develops his own speech ability by emitting sounds. He then fits them in again and again, both acoustically and rhythmically, and learns from this experience.

Just as with a baby, stimulation of the near senses (skin sensitivity, feeling for one's body and for movement, balance, taste) is, from the point of view of developmental psychology, of greater importance for a toddler in his second year than the promotion of the far senses (smell, sight, hearing). The latter does not get interesting for the child until his third year of life.

An Overview of Sensory Perception in the Second and Third Year of Life

1. Acoustic Perception

◆ The child is capable of differentiating between vocal signals of emotion (gentleness, fear), loud and quiet, as well as high and low tones, various types of voices (people, animals), long and short word pronunciations.
◆ Singing encourages the child's feeling for rhythm, and his language capacity.

2. Optic Perception

◆ Focussing on objects in various situations.
◆ Playing with objects promotes eye-hand coordination.

3. Tactile Perception

◆ Experiencing sensory impressions on the skin—warm and cold, rough and smooth, sharp and blunt, wet and dry.
◆ The most important organs of touch are the hands' skin receptors (no longer the mouth).
◆ The process of *grasping* and *handling*.

4. Kinesthetic Perception

◆ Developing the abilities to unconsciously control and steer body movements.
◆ Perception of body changes, (e.g. stretching one's arms).
◆ Coordinated and confident movements occur proprioceptively.
◆ Supports education, awareness of one's own body scheme, its limits and abilities.
◆ Keeping balance becomes more stable (organ of balance in inner ear, postural reflexes, and eyes regulate and control the body in posture, position and movement).
◆ Position-room orientation develops (one brings oneself into contact with other persons and objects).

2.3 Relationship and Speech Behavior—from Autonomy Up to the Strive for Independence

A toddler's emotional development in the second and third years of his life is characterized by the process of moving away from his direct "trust persons."

In the process of independent movement, and thus also movement away from his mother and/or father, a child starts, on the one hand, to drift away at the beginning of his second year of life. On the other hand however, he gets afraid and seeks protection as soon as these persons disappear out of his vision, or his plans are unsuccessful.

There is an interplay between this desire for freedom of movement and independence on the one hand, and the search for closeness and protection of his loved ones on the other.

The child tends to cling a lot and is afraid of being left alone (*fear of separation phase*). Towards the end of the second year, however, (from 18 months onwards) the child appears to be self-confident. More and more conflicts take place between the toddler (in his bid to gain independence) and his parents (as they try to set boundaries).

Assertiveness disputes are the result (*defiant phase*) here as long as it is not possible to make patient compromises, even without a wide language base. At the end of the third year of life, these emotional outbursts ease off; the child learns to put aside his own needs, and solutions can be reached more and more often with the use of language.

Compared with a baby, a toddler expresses various feelings from as early as 12-15 months (e.g. anger, jealousy, affection and rejection). He gets angry as soon as he is disturbed at work (playing, discovering). On the other hand, he likes to communicate by pointing out or demonstrating.

Social behavior, such as sharing or giving an object to someone, is relatively good. In the defiant age that follows, the child wants to assert his own opinion and frequently reacts angrily and furiously when this does not seem to work. Clear rules and the parents' good example help to give the child some orientation.

At the age of two to two-and-a-half the child occasionally appears to be already very independent (e.g. eating), he does, however, need constant help. This unstoppable urge to do things independently can also cause him to overtax himself, however, and this in turn leads to jealousy, clinging, and the need for soothing protection from his parents.

By the age of three, he is mature enough to make friends, and learns to follow stories that are read to him. He is thus ripe enough for kindergarten.

A toddler's speech development begins in the second year of life with *gesture language*. By pointing out and giving sounds, he attracts attention to his needs. From a lingual aspect, he begins formulating syllables such as ma-ma, ba-ba. This vocabulary is extended with the

help of parental interplay, such as naming objects and persons, and playing pointing games for word associations (e.g. tea, ball, car).

One-word sentences become *two-word sentences* between one-and-a-half and two years of age. It takes a good while for the child to identify his own name with the *I form*.

Children use this "I form" between the age of two and two-and-a-half. Simple conversations, asking questions, using positional adverbs (in front of, behind, under, on) and formulation of needs (e.g. hunger) become more frequent.

2.4 Playing and Learning Behavior–from Imitating and Performing to Trying Things Out Oneself

"Children's games are not games,
they are their most serious actions"

(MONTAIGNE)

Playing and *learning* are inseparably connected with each other at this age. Both terms could actually be used synonomously here. Every movement, every action is quite distinctive and new during this phase, i.e. every activity, whether playing or learning, is a building brick in the child's physical and mental development.

A toddler's motor learning activities in the second year of life are based mainly on his *need to imitate,* and thus his *facial sense* exploration.

At the beginning of his second year (12-15 months), the toddler tries to imitate his family's household and personal hygiene habits with his body, his gestures, facial expression and language. At 15-18 months, he has more endurance at play (up to 15 minutes), characterized by repetition and a series of actions. Popular games for toddlers up to two years of age are sticking shapes into the right holes, jigsaws and building towers (4-8 blocks on top of each other).

At the age of two to two-and-a-half, a toddler begins to tackle amounts, sizes, weights and spatial relationships by grouping (e.g.according to size), sorting (e.g.according to color) and by transferring (e.g. piece per piece). He develops his imagination in his first role plays (e.g. with dolls or toy animals) and his creative building experiments become three-dimensional constructions between the age of two-and-a-half and three.

Playing for a child means working in order to learn. In his first year of life, he played primarily with his body; in his second year he occupies himself with objects, including a high level of locomotion, known as *functional play*. The child develops his imagination spontaneously and without any pressure. He runs, hops, pulls and pushes, and is all the time motivated by social contact, i.e. he seeks proximity to others, but he also likes observing (*parallel play*).

Learning is always a *social process* with alternate exchanges of experience. Due to his extended vocabulary, double-signal information e.g. a spoken word together with the appropriate suitable gesture or facial expression, now gain in importance.

The quality of a child's actions continues improving in the third year of life. The child practices on and with objects or other children, tries out and assesses his physical skills, experiences new things and makes use of his mental and creative abilities. Depending on his disposition and the supportive opportunities available, the child works on and expands his own skillfulness and independence.

There are four initiative methods for learning elementary movements:

◆ Situative Learning: The learning process is set in motion with situations and behavior, in the form of physical and mental challenges and specific movement commands.

◆ Practice of elementary self-education by the motivation to learn and success of learning:
Children are not born completely without skillfulness; they need opportunities
   ◆ to move in all directions
   ◆ to repeat, so as to learn through experience
   ◆ to make use of their own emerging driving power

◆ There's no such thing as too early—introduction to learning and goal of learning:
It's a particularly good idea to consciously offer children opportunities, objects, instruments etc. as early as possible, in order to school their skillfulness, movement combination, and movement memory.

◆ Improvement in performance without pressure through support and encouragement, not through making demands on the child:
Movements become more fluid; the child feels strengthened, gains confidence and is encouraged to carry out more new movements when he is made aware of his actions through personal words of affection; the quality of his actions is confirmed by words of praise.

2.5   Hygienic Behavior–Growing Away from a Diaper

A toddler's active skills expand to include food intake, and then emptying of bladder and intestine during the second and third year of life.

Well-developed neuronal structures, and the child's own drive to fulfill the requirements of the entire situation are essential if a child is to assume certain habits regarding nutrition and hygiene.

As opposed to the normal routines at home, a child requires a further phase of orientation when in new places. As far as the situation in a swimming pool is concerned, a potty at the edge of the pool can help to support the child in his toilet-training. It is generally not until the third year of life that a child has the desire to use the actual toilet.

A baby empties his bladder as a reflex, and very often (approx. 30x per day) as soon as this little bladder is full.

His neural development means that at some time between the age of six and twelve months this frequency of urination decreases due to unconscious restraint. This habit becomes even more evident in the second year of life when the feeling of *needing to pass water* develops at the same time.

Towards the end of his second year of life, a child can control his sphincter muscles sufficiently, and seems to notice his need to urinate or empty his bowels.

His need to urinate drops to about 10x per day. By the fourth year of a toddler's life, his bladder has reached such a capacity that he can arbitrarily pass water even when his bladder is only slightly full, or else he can hold on.

Proper hygienic control does not begin until the age of 3-4 years.

According to statistical findings, *bowel control* exists for 97% of all children at the age of three. 90% of children don't achieve *bladder control* (during the day and at night) until the age of five.

The necessary maturity in the child's mental perception of his own cleanliness is usually reached at this age, as well. The child has then developed a sense of order, and has overcome the critical point up to the concept of property; he notices his bladder or intestine tensing up, and finds wet underwear uncomfortable.

Regardless of outside commands, the child wishes to develop an act of behavior which gives him a confident feeling of being aware of his needs, being able to express this need, and emptying his bladder etc. by himself.

This is a complex development, and it is based on his motivation to do it himself, his perceptive skills, and finally his ability to allocate this process into the entire situation.

2.6   Noticeable Movement Defects and Disturbances in Perception

This section looks at a range of movement defects and disturbances in perception, and gives advice on particular measures in parent-child lessons.

As movement development is an individual and variable process for each child, it is generally difficult to decide when a child's movements are *normal* or *faulty*[7]. When many children move around together in a group, it is much easier to observe individual characteristics.

The parents' insights are decisive here; they know their child better than anyone through being constantly around him. They are aware of his situation-specific behavior, and if they are unsure about something here, they should talk to the course instructor or children's doctor in order to be able to help their child as early as possible, and in the appropriate way.

As medical examinations checking a child's development are generally not carried out on children between two and four years of age[8], parents should get the advice of an expert if certain developmental impedients do arise. In this way and without much effort or bother, certain forms of movement can be deliberately promoted, and these have both a preventative and therapeutic influence. Basically, what holds is the following:

The earlier any deviations are identified, and the more specific the counteractive therapy is, the more likely it is to succeed, and therefore also reduce the backwardness in development.

---

7   One distinguishes between the child who is *weak and doesn't move much* (quiet, likes playing on his own, easy, unproblematic child), the child who is *restless and can't concentrate* (fidgety, permanently on the move, explores briefly, plays for a short while, likes charging about outside, a demanding child), and the child that is *oversensitive* to movement and being moved (has difficulties with all actions, is clumsy, avoids all forms of movement).

8   Check-up 7 for toddlers up to 24 months, check-up 8 for children over 43 months.

If movement defects or disturbances in perception do arise in this period of development, these disturbances in taking in, passing on or processing stimuli, are all expressed in the brain.

They may stem from the sensory organs (e.g. over/under sensitive eyes, ears), or from the brain (e.g. lack of oxygen before, during or after the birth, premature birth, minimal brain hemorrhage).

Information is taken in by seven sensory systems:

1. Tactile system: Stimulus of movement and touch is taken in via the skin surface. It reacts protectively (*protopathic*) and judgmentally (*epicritical*). Depth sensitivity means that the place of touch, pressure or vibration is exactly identified.

2. Balance or vestibular system: Visual and positional stimuli are combined and control muscular tension.[9] If it is not possible to keep visual hold of an object/situation, this is a sign of a disturbance in visual sense; the child cannot process what he has seen.

3. Proprioceptive or kinesthetic system: The perception and awareness of one's own movements occurs via touching of and pressure on muscles, tendons and joints, and is passed on. In keeping with body structure and the awareness of the body's outer boundaries (body scheme), the next movement process is determined and realistically planned.

4. Visual system: The eyes identify the object (foreground and background differentiation), the form constancy (identify type of object), its spatial position (down, up, at the front, at the back, sidewards) and spatial relationships.

5. Acoustic system: This works in two different ways. While the ears gather hearing impressions, the mouth forms tones of speech.[10]

6. Taste system: The type of surface, texture and taste of materials are examined and distinguished in the mouth, using the taste nerves on the tongue.

7. Smelling system: Smells are perceived by the nose, and are then distinguished and evaluated according to type (sweet, acidic, mild, spicy, pleasant etc.).

All these sensory impressions[11] are brought together in the brain, i.e. this is where the so-called *sensory integration* occurs, which enables us to learn and react appropriately.

Difficulties in learning occur when
◆ it is not possible to differentiate between important things and non-important things.
◆ unwanted sensory stimuli cannot be blocked out or filtered and the brain is inundated. Permanent *distraction* makes long-term preoccupation with something impossible.
◆ the quality of the stimuli is insufficiently taken in by the senses.
◆ Stimulus information is not recognized, and not coordinated.[12]

The most common disturbances in perception in the first years of life are:
◆ Disturbances in basic muscular tension (muscle tonus is too high or too low). One differentiates between *hypotonic* (limp, flabby) and hypertonic (overstretched) children. Whereas the first group of children may be described as being over-mobile, weak in posture, awkward, slow, feeble and slow to react, the second group's movements tend to be tense (particularly their fine motor actions), stiff, lacking in rhythm and harmony, rough and too broad. Both hyper- and hypotonic children tire quickly, and this leads to a dislike of movement. For hypotonic children, movement is an effort, and they dislike it. They avoid movement, and are not willing to make an effort, with the consequence that their motor development is

---

9   80% of children with developmental disturbances have difficulties controlling their balance.
10 70% of children with delayed speech development have disturbances in the processing done by their basic senses.
11 The seven senses are divided up according to their meaning as *near senses* (basic senses) where the body is in contact with the stimulus source (the hand's sense of touch, sense of balance in the inner ear maze, sense of movement in muscles, tendons and joints, sense of taste in the tongue and palate) and the *far senses* where the source of stimulus is further away from the body (seeing, listening, smelling). Well-integrated near senses form the basis for an optimal development of the far senses.
12 Coordinating sensory perception begins at the age of 3-4 months. At 8-9 months, chronological and spatial stimulus information is identified, stored, put into action, and consciously repeated (e.g. knocking building blocks against each other).

impeded. Practical help in the form of fast and strong movements in upright position counteract this. They build up muscle tonus (e.g. by hopping, rollicking, turning, climbing and throwing heavy objects.) Long, careful and conscious movements in relaxed body positions reduce muscle tonus (e.g. swinging, fine motor games with shapes and sizes, massage).

◆ Disturbances in the combining work of muscle groups, muscle chains, and parts of the body (*low coordination*). They can clearly be seen when certain movements of the body or parts of the body are not in tune with each other, and cannot be carried out separately (disassociated); unwanted, so-called *associated movements,* occur instead. This is also the case when both halves of the cerebrum, each responsible for the opposite side of the body, do not work accurately with each other. At toddler age, it is already possible to observe the three most significant areas of coordination: *hand-hand coordination* (e.g. when clapping, threading pearls), *eye-hand coordination* (e.g. when building towers, throwing at targets), and *hand-foot coordination* (pedalling and steering a tricycle, climbing). Up to his 18th month, a child should not prefer using a particular side most of the time, so that cross movements (e.g. when crawling) can enable an equal build-up of both sides, and the child can move in a steady direction. Later on, the *lateralization process* begins where one of the two cerebral sections is activated to a greater extent. *Handedness* is a process of development which continues on until the fifth year of life.

◆ Disturbances when taking in experiences in regards to amounts and direction (*attention—concentration*). This is particularly noticeable when the child has had too much stimulus; he keeps on getting distracted, he hardly listens, does not carry out any activity with interest, but rather frequently changes activity and then tires quickly. A good idea here is to bind him with strong body contact (perhaps massage), consciously give him only a few toys to play with, look after and care for him with definite daily routines, get him accustomed to certain rituals, work out clear methods of action, and learn to stick to them. In this way, the child experiences the support that he needs, his orientation improves, and he gains in self-confidence. Simple, changing impulses enable a *hyperactive child* to learn how to control himself (e.g. by twirling with changes in direction, running with stops along the way).

◆ Disturbances in tactile perception (*tactile oversensitivity*). Due to weaknesses in the central nervous line of stimulus, touching is perceived to be unpleasant. As the stimulus threshold is very low here, one should avoid subjecting such children to sudden changes in position. Extremely gentle treatment and touching while cuddling, carrying and swinging, and gradual stroking of different materials (sponge, brush etc.) help to break down this oversensitivity. After that, one must try to school his perception of touch, e.g by playing in limited areas (tunnel of mats), playing naked, walking barefooted, twirling and swinging on his parent's lap, and games with other children. Normality can then return.

◆ Disturbances in brain function (*minimal cerebral dysfunction = MCD*), a collective term for for slight discrepancies in movement and perception which accompany the defects already mentioned above, e.g. reduced capacity of information intake, low memory functions, weaknesses in processing visual, auditive, tactile-kinesthetic and vestibular information, connective problems, difficulties with central integration, or a lack in feedback control mechanisms. They appear in the form of hyperactivity, motor defects and retarded speech.

3 Parents and Course Instructors

3.1 The Parental Role in the Process of a Child's Personality Development

"Parents should see themselves as the child's partner, i.e. they should motivate and encourage him, but be encouraged and motivated by him, as well."

(DIEM)

In the process of a child's development, his emotions may change suddenly, a situation which the parents should always be prepared for in their behavior to their child. At the beginning of his second year of life (13-16 months), a toddler is quite a moody person. On the one hand he seeks close personal contact; on the other hand, he puts up a fight and no longer wants to be held and carried. He then in turn looks to his parents for support of his actions. His body language makes it difficult to understand his needs.

By the age of 17-20 months, a child has learned how to attract his parents' attention, and he tries to control this with both positive and negative behavior. This early phase of defiance demands pedagogical empathy from his parents, i.e. by offering their child stimulating and interesting ideas to occupy himself with, while at the same time encouraging him to look for solutions by himself.

Up to the age of two years (21-24 months), a child often refuses to *cooperate*. One must try and break this barrier. When the child is given the opportunity to *help out*, without actually specifying the tasks (e.g. in the household, packing the swimming gear, taking his clothes off), the child feels involved; he can make use of his knowledge, and he is needed. Praise and recognition are always of pedagogical use, as are words of reprimand when necessary.

From 25-28 months, a child generally has balanced behavior. He is active and full of life. He becomes more independent, and is stubborn when he senses the controlling intervention of his parents.

The toddler's role behavior in swimming lessons changes, too as he continuously becomes more and more independent (29-32 months); a fact that both the parents and the swimming instructor must take into consideration. It is recommended that beginners go into a separate group in order to make fitting in and orientation easier for them, and not to overtax them. Later on, the child knows what to expect, how the lesson runs and he is familiar with the course instructor, and the other group members. He can sit quietly, listen and wait, and is happy when he has fulfilled his tasks, particularly when the instructor has praised him.

Once the child has gotten used to the course instructor, he then subordinates himself. He is more willing to accept criticism from this person than from his parents. He often proudly shows his parents his newly acquired skills, which is a clear sign of how his role is changing. The child wants to be liked by his admirers, he does, however, feel under slight pressure when he doesn't succeed in some task.

The rise in the child's self-education and independent actions means that the parents become escort persons (*audience and assistant role*). They also work as *interpreters* for certain game ideas or set tasks, including those with other participants, i.e. the group or instructor. They help their child carry out movements, ensure his safety, and give him words of encouragement. In this new role, the parents must consciously motivate, comfort and encourage him, and not exert pressure or judge him.

From the third year on, the child needs his parents as *playing partners*. This makes the game even more stimulating. As the child is now capable of comprehending what he has observed and can put verbal explanations into practice, the parents assume a significant role of setting example (*parents model behavior*). Just how intensively they do intervene, i.e. how attentive and active they are in the lesson themselves, how positive their reaction is to the water, and how they are integrated into the group, are all factors which can positively influence and support what goes on in the lesson.

If the child appears to be indecisive towards the lesson, it is a good idea to let him watch the activities around him first. His father and/or mother should pointedly participate in the lesson, and arouse the child's willingness. After having thought about it for a while, he will then come out of isolation and get involved.

The initial unsureness and inner refusal among new beginners generally disappears after four lessons. Here and there a child may refuse to fulfill a task in the middle of a lesson. Again, as above, it is advisable to wait first before trying out alternative tasks. A brief *time-out* with a break (waiting on the pool steps or outside the pool) is only a suitable solution in exceptional cases.

3.2 The Course Instructor as an Advisor, a Creative Designer, and the Person to Whom Toddler and Parents Relate

The course instructor is both an expert and pedagogical advisor.

First of all, one must pay attention to certain conditions, and that every child is always addressed by his name, as this illustrates the openness of the lesson. Contact is intensified when the child is occasionally carried into the water by the course instructor. As the child's comprehension of language grows, particularly in the third year, the better the understanding works between course instructor and child.

If a child is to be successfully guided through a lesson, it is necessary to have information about his development.

This is provided by the list of attendance among other things, in which the reasons for absence from the course are explained. When then the course instructor explains the *contents* of how to promote a child's development, offers the parents advice on the grip, water accustomization and diving techniques, these must all be conveyed appropriate to the child's development. Any questions that may arise are to be answered with explanation.

Due to the frequent fluctuations in a child's moods—particularly in the second year of life—movement ideas, games and activities should always have several possible solutions at hand, so as to be able to vary the run of events in such a way that the children can understand. The *degree of difficulty of the tasks* must be selected and adjusted to fit in with the child's current performance levels in such a way that the children are always the *discoverers*.

The course instructor is there to arouse the children's interest and willingness, and create movement tasks which are manageable for them. The trick is the right dosage: if the demands are too high, the child will be quick to give up (fear of lack of success).

This is particularly true in the third year of a child's life when he is able to mentally structure and estimate his plans. If he is given time to repeat movements, he will gather more courage. If the task is too easy, however, the child's interest dwindles as the incentive is missing; he starts to play around, and turns away again.

For this reason, a type of circuit training (different tasks at each station) has proven to be very successful from a methodical point of view, as this is full of variety and is something for everybody. Each child can make good use of his current interests. The more steadily and confidently a child develops with these exercises, the more he will ask for them again.

If materials and aids are used, one must take their purpose and effect into consideration beforehand: *equipment* must be of a *challenging nature*.

The course instructor must be sure to take into account the following points:

◆ Support the parent-child relationship in a trustful way.
◆ Encourage the children with their parents to move the appropriate way (speaking to them, demonstrating).
◆ Have a structure, and a clear run of events in your lesson; be of assistance; take safety measures; prepare apparatus and materials and be flexible when implementing them; ensure that safety rules are obeyed, if not, intervene.
◆ Bring the group together; let them lose their inhibitions, and encourage them to help each other.
◆ Intervene as seldom as possible to correct errors, but offer movement support instead. An instructor should be capable of carrying out a task in methodical steps.
◆ Involve children and parents in the lesson with task activities, e.g. using them for a variety of jobs (parent language, child language) or for special safety positions.
◆ Encourage or calm down the parents when the child's behavior is taxing their nerves; confront such situations with feeling and understanding.
◆ Do not announce tasks until *all* participants are paying attention. Speak slowly and clearly. Use the child's minor vocabulary as a yardstick.
◆ Give parents and children enough time and opportunity to get accustomed to a piece of equipment *before* the actual activity.

◆ Take into account the following methodical teaching aspect: the younger the child, the more often it is necessary to change activity, place, and form of organization with short waiting periods in between.

◆ The course instructor always speaks eye-to-eye with children and parents; otherwise he will not get through to them, nor get the desired level of attention.

4 Toddler Swimming

4.1 The Meaning Behind and Objectives of Movement, Play and Sport for Todddlers

"A healthy child always wants to be active. Give the child things to do; these are the best gifts of all. The child can't rest at all; he wants work tasks!"

(FRÖBEL)

Physical and mental difficulties and weaknesses that arise later on in life can often be traced back to early childhood. Our lifestyle, living conditions, the ever-progressive mechanization and automation at the cost of well-balanced physical exercise in our free time (car instead of bike, TV instead of going for a walk), often threaten our healthy way to live.

In order to prevent numerous illnesses of the cardiovascular and breathing systems, metabolic disturbances, autonomic control disturbances, weaknesses of the muscles, ligaments, connective tissue and posture, as well as defects in motor coordination—all due to a lack of movement—it is necessary to counteract these symptoms with the promotion of suitable movement.

One has to use organized movement and play opportunities to encourage and prophylactically strengthen the child's development, skills and entire personality.

Early movement in water enhances the children's physical state of health and their motor activity. It encourages them to enjoy movement, and lets them work on their social behavior within a group. The significance of water accustomization in the form of preparatory exercises before learning to swim, so as to get the children familiar with water, is a fact that we are aware of from the *basic teaching methods* when working with non-swimmers. The development of sports, movement and day-to-day culture in general, but also specifically parent-child swimming, should be looked at from an integral and *multi-perspective* angle. Moving in water is no longer limited to the sport aspect, but rather offers scope for play and pleasure, relaxation and compensatory elements, fitness and therapy, social and physical contact. Toddler swimming enables children to carry out intensive movement with their parents with close physical contact, and to experience and discover together a medium which stimulates body, senses and movement.

The most important objectives
◆ Letting the children realize their desire of movement, and giving them enough time, understanding, and scope for this need.
◆ Contribution to the child's healthy, independent, free and relaxed development.
◆ Intensification of the parent-child relationship through skin contact, common experience, and strengthening of mutual trust.
◆ Strengthening of the cardiovascular and respiratory systems[13], as well as of the bone, ligament and muscular apparatus, in order to prevent respiratory weaknesses, or limitations of the locomotor systems.
◆ Completion of coordination, balance and body control through stimulating, bilateral movements.
◆ Improvement of posture, and prevention of foot weaknesses by strengthening muscles and making joints more supple.
◆ Making the children more sensitive to sensory and physical perception.
◆ Energy development and physical compensation for mental performances.
◆ Initiation/practice/promotion of social behavior and social skills with movement games within the group.
◆ Getting the children accustomed to the medium of water and preparation for basic forms of movement in the water-coping phase.
◆ Regulation of the child's sleeping behavior and appetite (secondary effect).

---

[13] Movement in warm, moist air is particularly recommended for children with asthma problems.

4.2 The Concept of Interactive Movement Stimulation–Exploring the Water World Together

A toddler is not able to swim, and due to his current state of development, is not able to identify and estimate danger. He is, therefore, dependent on his parents' protection and accompaniment. He can receive the best stimulation to try out and learn new things from his parents or within a group. In the process of togetherness, the advantage in the group is that all participants are interested in the same thing, i.e. to get contact with others, to meet for collective activity, and to support each other. There is a variety of interactive possibilities.

Children play beside or with other children, parents communicate with each other. The group, as individuals supporting each other in the community, experiences in lesson form how the course instructor's activities are accepted by both the children and the parents; they are tried and tested together, and then developed further by themselves.

Toddlers have high demands: they demand a lot of attention, enjoy an audience and praise, and develop in independence, almost to doggedness. Then, they look for role models for orientation and learning. During their discoveries, they bravely test their boundaries, and at the same time seek shelter and protection when they need someone to lean on.

This mutual experience in the water makes parents more aware of their child's *individuality* and *uniqueness*. Through constant visual and physical contact, the child feels their attention and feels confident and contented.

Swimming aids are generally not intended for use in lessons. Skin contact, communication, playing with, and paying attention to each other are elements which should be practiced unrestrictedly, as a child experiences his bonding abilities particularly in his first three years of life. The parents, meanwhile, learn more and more about their child's skills as they carry out, and experience things together, and observe him constantly. They feel encouraged to allow him more scope as his sense of independence continues to develop.

4.3   Learning of Movement and Swimming Behavior

The process of learning motor skills occurs in three steps: *gross coordination, fine coordination, and finest coordination.* Gross coordination centers around the processing of information. Acts of movement must be planned, as they are initially new. These procedures are often still unsuccessful, have to be repeated, and altered. A toddler needs a relatively long time to process new information, as well as a high, and as yet, uneconomical strength effort to carry out the movements. His series of partial movements is still not fluid, but rather jerky with indefinite breaks, acceleration and deceleration are strung together instead. This phase of functional development is known as the *cognitive phase.*

The less amount of attention needed when repeating a movement, the more capacity there is for combining it with other movements. A fluid movement process comes to light, and the child begins to mentally anticipate other movements. Frequent repetition and variation of movements result in flexible patterns and rhythms of movement, as well as new muscular possibilities of control. The *associative phase* begins when a movement can be carried out fluidly, combined and flexibly designed to comply with situational conditions.

In his second year of life, a child practices and improves his movements by repeating and satisfying his *functional desire* (open door, close door—light on, light off—fill with water, empty water out). Movement becomes a means to an end. In the third year, many movements (balancing, jumping down) contain an exciting element of unsureness as far as the result is concerned, combined with the feeling of relief of having his feet on solid ground, or being caught by his parents. The child learns by trying and testing; experiences sensitize sensory perception. Fine coordination and confidence improve.

The *autonomic phase,* i.e. finest coordination, does not come for many years.It is only then that the attention a child pays to carrying out a movement action can be transferred to the objective of the action.

For children between the 19th and 24th month, a complete chain of movement in the form of movement skills (jumping, diving, moving under water, pulling oneself up, and holding on to the edge) only exists in exceptional cases. Most toddlers could show individual parts of this *chain of movement*, but were not able to swim.This was especially due to the fact that they could not lift up their head to take in air when in prone position.

The development of leg movements throughout the first 20 months of life were recorded using tracer streak photos, and were described in two phases. In the first phase (3-11 months), about 80% of movements are steered by reflex or emotions. In the second phase (11-20 months), leg movements are controlled arbitrarily. In the first year of life, depending on age and state of development, a child's legs can kick and thrust parallel to each other, as well as in alternation. The child's body is mainly in flat prone position supported by his parent's hand. A child in his second year of life wants to move around in water in vertical position. The legs are always moved in alternation.

Depending on age and the state of development, there is a change in the angles at the hips, knees and ankles. At the beginning, one could describe the form of movement as "stomping", later as "heel-on," and finally as "cycling". These movements do not produce any propulsion initially. They only become considerably stronger in the third year, and due to the child's urge to lie in prone position again, become significantly more effective; the movements at this stage have been known as "dog paddling" or as the first step towards learning the so-called "human stroke."

This process fits in with the theories on motor learning development at toddler age which have been derived from observations and personal accounts:

1. Adaptive Learning: The child learns by moving and being moved.

2. Perceptive Learning: The child learns movement by directing his attention, and becoming aware of the movement. The learning process is one of active understanding. Even if the sensory impressions are not yet reflected, the impressions themselves are already registered.

3. Active Learning: The child playfully tries out movements and attempts variations; these are all then developed into skills. At the point of resistance, his desire to attempt things and solve his own tasks increases even more. By trying things out himself, the child boosts his own ego, and learns where his limits are.

4. Comprehensible Learning: From the third year of life, the child develops an interest in how and why movement occurs; he gains insight. He explores the mechanism of objects with curiosity, and questions cause and effect.

Other classic learning models for toddler age supplemented these theories:

1. Model Learning: The child observes movements made by persons, animals or dolls, and imitates these movements.

2. Learning by Reinforcement (operative conditioning): The child is motivated by praise to continue practicing and learning.

3. Learning by Signals (stimulus-reaction learning): After a verbal signal ("1-2-3"), the child learns to concentrate on a movement, and to react (e.g. to jump from the edge of the pool).

4. Avoidance Learning: If a movement is regularly forbidden, the child learns to refrain from doing it.

5. Learning by Trial and Error: By testing his own skills and abilities, successful and ineffective attempts teach the child the best way to get around a situation.

Learning is based on processing experiences founded on the development of associative patterns (ideas) through stimulus linking and combination, or the classicification of information (cluster formation).

In the second year of life movement, learning through movement is triggered by
◆ curiosity about how things work
◆ imitation and repetition
◆ motivation—confirmation of achievements with words of encouragement and praise
◆ scope and opportunities to play with a lot of variety.

As his speech comprehension improves, and his desire to explore his environment, and to play with other children grows, too, the toddler practices
◆ consciously complying with movement commands
◆ learning how to solve the problems of movement tasks.

In the initial role of the observer, he watches other persons' movements, compares them, and puts them into practice.

4.4 Research Findings, Anticipated Success, and the End Results: And When Does the Child Finally Learn to Swim?

The findings of the MUKi[14] study about the influence of baby swimming on motor development in the first year of life, clearly indicates that body posture and balance abilities can be improved through swimming. Furthermore, regular participation, the parents' attitude and behavior toward body contact and swimming, proved to have an incredibly significant influence here.

A study comparing toddlers of an average age of 18 months came to the conclusion that those children with water experience[15] were more familiar with their handling of the water. This was particularly noticeable while washing hands or showering at/under a jet of water.

Differences between the parent groups could also be detected: parents of "swimmer" children were more comfortable in the water than those whose children had no water experience. This can imply a process of water accustomization on one hand, and a difference in interests and lower level of parental motivation, on the other.

Another study looked at the effects of early stimulation on the development of a child in his third and fourth year of life, and also established influences which encourage a child's personality development, e.g.better situative adaptiveness, higher level of self-confidence and independence. They put these facts down to early experience with movement and promotion of independence.

One study verified that development deficits, and lack of body control among children living in institutions were able to be rectified at toddler age through movement programs and games in water. He pointed out the importance of furthering gross motor skills, social contact and speech behavior.

---

14 "Motorische Untersuchung von Kindern im ersten Lebensjahr" = the examination of children's motor activity in the first year of life

15 Regular participation in baby swimming at the age of three months

Just exactly what successes are achievable at toddler age depends, to a great extent, on regular participation, the arrangement of lesson atmosphere, the lesson content—appropriate to the child's development—given by a motivated instructor, cooperation of the parents, and last but not least, the child's experiences to date.

Toddlers who have already taken part in baby swimming courses can be expected to develop the following skills in water (in a cumulative form) up to their third year of life:

◆ Keeping their balance in prone and supine position with a parent's hand supporting from underneath.
◆ Keeping their balance in prone and supine position with the help of equipment (e.g. boards) in their hands.
◆ Changeover from prone to supine position, and coming upright out of prone position into vertical position.
◆ Turning in vertical position with changes in direction.
◆ Diving and pulling oneself up without help.
◆ Forward movement with alternate leg strokes in prone and supine position with swimming aids or the support of a parent's hand.
◆ Arm movements (a mole digging, a dog paddling) done simultaneously with leg movements after verbal signals.
◆ Moving hand over hand along the edge of the pool.
◆ Being accustomed to water, showing no unsure or fearful reactions to the water-pouring test or water splashes, pouring water over his own head.
◆ Gliding to the pool edge, and pulling themselves up.
◆ Hanging onto the edge of the pool, and breathing out underwater.
◆ Hanging onto the edge of the pool, and diving down.
◆ Removing one hand from the edge, turning around and pushing oneself away from the edge.
◆ Diving for objects in water that they can stand up in (e.g. on the steps).
◆ Jumping on a command: "1-2-3" and diving under.
◆ Sliding, swimming a 1-3m distance under water to parents' hands.
◆ Swimming piggy-back on their parent's back, above and below water.

Yardsticks for newcomers, for the period of time that they require to cope with this learning challenge, are as follows: their experiences to date in the bath, how they get on in groups and in new situations, the parents' attitude to water, and the child's disposition and willingness to learn. The child himself always determines the work tempo, so as to feel safe in the water, to accept or refuse help from his parents, and to come to grips with the situation.

The question as to when a child can learn how to swim depends on his physical, motor, cognitive, emotional and social development. Decisive factors here are particularly the state of development of his central nervous system, his concentration abilities, his ability to actually cope with the water, his understanding of tasks and the amount of movement experience he has. This level of maturity and willingness to learn is generally only to be expected to appear at the age of 5-6.

III The Practical Side Of Toddler Swimming

5 The Planning and Organization of a Course

5.1 Planning and Carrying Out a Course

Parent-child courses for toddlers in the second and third year of life require exact planning, i.e. the groups must be formed according to age, ability and state of learning, so that each participant feels comfortable, and in correspondence with his level of experience.

Toddler swimming courses are by no means to be seen as a direct continuation of baby courses: many parents only start coming to swim with their children at this age, and are therefore, in some cases, inexperienced with water, groups and lessons.

From an organizational aspect, it is advisable to make enrollment lists for *beginner* and *follow-up* courses, and plan to divide them up according to approximate age groups in a sensible way. This also depends on the amount of enrollments (e.g. 13-18, 19-24, 24-30, 30-36 months).

At the age of 18 months, children are generally able to walk. After that, they need a lot of free space for their own actions; at 24 months, their willingness to imitate is well-developed, as is their speech comprehension, and ability to express themselves from 30 months onwards.

For this reason, the course instructor must plan his lessons according to the child's level of development, and can then organize and design a tailor-made lesson with the help of demonstration with group tasks or verbal instructions.

The ideal group size for a lesson would be eight parent-child couples, not taking into account other factors, such as the size of the pool, financial handicaps, supervision facilities, material circumstances.

Brothers or sisters should not take part in the lesson as a parent's duty is the permanent supervision of this child, too. The introduction of childcare facilities or events which run parallel to the swimming lesson are good.

Whether as a closed enrollment course or an open enrollment course going on for a year, the lessons should always be set up in blocks of about 10 lessons lasting 45 minutes. A lesson of this length is long enough to plan a general aim and build in different emphasis activities beforehand, and then proceed in steps from lesson to lessson.

One must plan a lesson thematically, but not dogmatically, dealing with the steps of progress as block-related, and not for each individual lesson. This ensures enough scope for development, takes account of unexpected circumstances, preserves the playful character of the lessons, and enables parents and their children to make constant progress in the water.

A method that has proven to be successful is picking out a particular topic, and then using only one playing object—but very intensively at that—and letting the children experiment with this object, and find out all the many things they can do with it (challenging their imagination!).

5.2   Information for Parents and Game Suggestions for Showering and Bathing at Home

A toddler is confronted with water more or less as part of his daily routine. Washing, showering, or taking a bath are all elements of our personal hygiene. A child can really get to like this routine, and not see it as a burden when he is allowed to peacefully enjoy looking after his body with and in water, without any time pressures, and with ample playing opportunities. Toys in the bath encourage the child to stay there for a while, older brothers and sisters show off their diving skills, a doll's hair is washed for demonstrative purposes, or his mother and father set an example for him of how relaxing bathing can be, and how uncomplicated showering and washing can be.

To enable stressfree bathing for both parents and children, one must pay attention to certain points:
◆ Do not wash, shower or bathe the child when he is overtired. This may end up in the child refusing to go into the water at a later stage.
◆ Washing, showering or bathing should always take place without time pressure, so as to encourage the feeling of contentedness.
◆ The subjective relationship to water (and at the same time to hygiene) can be improved when washing is not a "must," but takes place in playful form.
◆ Toddlers wish to be actively involved in bathing and showering as in all other activities. Therefore, give the child something to do, on his own and with others.
◆ Bathing should go on for no longer than 30 minutes to prevent the skin from losing its necessary fat layer. If the child wishes to come out earlier, then comply with this wish.
◆ An anti-slipping mat can be placed into the bath. A showering curtain prevents unwanted flooding and the child can splash away as he pleases.
◆ Bathing substances should not be added to the water. Shortly before leaving the water one can clean the child's body with soap if necessary.

◆ Needless to say, the child should never be allowed to stay in the bath without supervision. Besides, bathing with mother, father or another child is generally more fun. At the same time, the child learns to handle himself, and the other naked bodies in a natural way.

◆ The child also requires suitable toys (in size and texture).

◆ Dry the body carefully (particularly areas with skin folds) with a soft towel, so as not to irritate the child's sensitive skin.

The following forms of play are suitable for a toddler:

◆ He can fill the bath, or some bowls using the shower attachment.

◆ He learns the different water temperatures (warm, cold).

◆ He can change the the power of the water jet.

◆ He may occasionally hold the shower attachment himself to shower down his body.

◆ He can sit paddling, and splashing with his hands and feet.

◆ He can be activated to kick his legs when lying on his stomach with a parent's hand or lower arm holding them underneath.

◆ In the same position as above, the child can be encouraged to blow into the water, to blubber, to dip under, and then look at his hands or some objects.

◆ When lying on his back supported by his parents' hands, he can be encouraged to put his head in the water.

5.3   Some Points of Advice for the Swimming Pool

The water should have a temperature of 32°C, and be about 1m 20 deep.

Ideally, the pool should have a bar, or overflow channel at the edge for the children to hold on to, wide steps on which exercises can be carried out when sitting down, standing up or under support, and a non-slip area at the edge for jumping into the water.

The children should not stay in the water for longer than 45 minutes. Depending, however, on the water temperature, the regulation of this temperature, the child's age, his movement intensity, and personal form on that particular day, this can be reduced where necessary.

Parents and children should stay up to their shoulders in water to prevent the children from cooling out with their wet skin.

The children should remain sitting and standing at the edge of the pool or on mats for a short time only, while constantly wetting those parts of the body which are not in the water. Waiting periods should be avoided when going from station to station.

It is necessary for a child to leave the water sooner when he has not had enough sleep, when he has just recovered from an illness, or when he is teething or hungry, as these all cause him to get cold sooner. A child that is feeling cold in the water is no longer interested in playing, and he clings onto his parent; his face changes colour; his hands and feet become pale, and he indicates or expresses his will to get out of the water.

For safety reasons, it is a good idea when communal changing rooms have lockable doors, diaper-changing facilities, a playpen and sealable diaper bins. These requirements are not always fulfilled, however.

One should make use of or instigate possibilities for the children to shower or bath by themselves. A bicycle tube over the showerhead serves as a shower attachment; the children can climb into basins or pots by themselves.

The swimming pool must have an emergency telephone, as well as a place for the swimming and playing equipment to dry out on.

5.4   Hygiene and the Prevention of Illness

Despite all the joys of swimming, there are of course dangers lurking, e.g. of unwanted injuries and illness due to incorrect behavior. A number of basic rules can prevent this. In a toddler swimming course, it is then the parents who must carefully stick to these rules.

Only toddlers who are feeling healthy can take part in swimming. Going swimming with sniffles is a matter of discretion that the parents themselves must answer. In this case, it is advisable to have tissues lying at the edge for cleaning the child's nose when necessary, and this warm and moist air encourages little noses to run even more. Diving under is not recommended here.

All users of the pool should either wear their hair back or put on a swimming cap (depending on pool rules), so as to avoid the unpleasantness of long hair swimming around in the water (and touching one's hand or mouth, in particular). Toddlers with long strands of hair at the front should keep this hair out of their face with a clip so as to prevent it from getting into their eyes, nose or mouth, and irritating the child after water-pouring or diving attempts.

Even with the health requirements laid down by the pool itself, all users of the pool must also play their part in preventing bacteria from spreading. This includes personal hygiene, beginning with an all-over shower (*without* clothes) before entering the pool. In the second year of life, when the toddlers are not yet steady when standing or walking, the parents should shower them in their arms. In the third year, the toddlers should take a shower or bath by themselves. Properly fitted bathing shoes prevent them from slipping.

As there is an increased desire to pass water immediately after leaving the pool, it is a good idea to get the child accustomed to a potty (clearly visible at the edge of the pool) and, during certain exercises (e.g. jumping in) when he is standing outside the pool, to occasionally ask him if he needs to pass water.

At the end of the lesson, one should head straight for the toilets, and then take off the wet swimming clothing. A warming bathrobe does a good job on the way to the showers.

Washing and bathing afterwards under the shower (with a hose working as a showerhead at a suitable height) and in the bath, becomes a very popular way to finish up the lesson the more regularly it occurs. Before getting into the water, one deliberately takes a lukewarm shower. After coming out of the water, the participants should take a warm shower however, as this quickens the body's warming up process.

Dressing and undressing a toddler is carried out in such a way as to adapt him to the surrounding temperatures, i.e. the *onion method*, so that the body gradually gets accustomed to the changes in temperature. Diapers can be changed on a warm bench or on isomats on the floor. Rolling the child to both sides here helps any water that has got into the toddler's ears to flow out again.

In warm rooms, the most important thing to put on first is the diaper; the remaining clothes can be put on again shortly before leaving the building, so as to prevent the toddler from overheating. Rubbing in lotion, or drinking warm tea helps the toddler to warm up in the colder seasons. When blow-drying their hair, always blow warm air towards the ears, as well. When leaving the building, the child should have his head covered as this keeps out draughts and prevents colds.

5.5 First Aid, the Duties of Care and Responsibility to a Child

This is an extremely important section, as knowledge of and familiarity with the appropriate treatment can save lives, even if such emergencies do seldom occur. Baby and toddler swimming courses stand and fall with the confidence of knowing how to react properly at the right time.

Preventive measures must be taken in the swimming pool, so as to be able to react quickly in the case of accidents and emergencies. For a course instructor to be able to provide help properly and quickly, it is imperative that he is familiar with *first aid* measures. Charity associations and children's hospitals offer first aid courses specifically focused on toddler first aid.

Before starting the lesson, it is necessary to check the pool area for any potential danger spots, to ensure the first aid cupboard is complete and that the telephone is in working order. Furthermore, one must know what rescue apparatus is available, where the emergency exits are, and which hospital is responsible for that area and can be contacted in the case of an emergency.

The course instructor has a duty of care and responsibility to his group for the duration of the lesson. This means that he informs the adults of possible dangers, intervenes when this advice is not heeded, checks areas of danger, and ensures that house rules and swimming regulations are obeyed. He is the first to enter the pool, and the last to get out.

Now and then during the lesson, it is necessary from a didactic aspect to also explain, demonstrate and assess from the side of the pool.

Parents (or those "trust persons" appointed to go swimming with the child) are fully responsible for their child. It is always necessary to find out whether there are non-swimmers or unsure swimmers among the parents. The instructor must pay special attention in this case, even if the water is shallow.

Legal responsibility for any damage occurring to persons or property during the lesson varies from institution to institution. The course instructor is recommended to clear up this issue beforehand with both the organizers and participants, or alternatively have an agreement in the course program or working contract. It goes without saying that every swimming instructor has to have liability insurance.

A course instructor must have so-called "limited" rescue abilities for the beginners' pool (depth of up to 1.35m). This includes (in Germany) having the bronze swimming badge (proof of one's ability to swim over 10 metres and dive 1.35m, to swim 200m within 7 minutes, as well as knowing the

swimming rules) and being able to give first aid. These tests are carried out by swimming and lifesaving associations, and the water watch division of the (German) Red Cross.

Statistically seen, accidents in swimming pools occur seldomly when compared with other types of sports, but they usually have more serious consequences. The main sources of danger are jumping (collision), running (danger of slipping), insufficient attentiveness and supervision by non-swimmers (swallowing water, submerging), the incorrect use of equipment, or existing organic weaknesses a person may have which one wasn't aware of beforehand.

A toddler, due to his motor independence in running and climbing, his curiosity and inability to survey situations and estimate risks, is at permanent risk of causing an accident or being involved in one. The typical accidents with toddlers are due to suffocation (when something has gone down the wrong way), poisoning or corrosion (from acids), scalding and burning, or falling injuries.

Below is a list of what can happen in toddler swimming courses, and how the course instructor can combat these dangers through an explanatory discussion with the parents, as well as through his own judicious behavior:

◆ *Falls* can occur during a diaper change, by slipping on the floor at the pool edge, outside the pool, or on the wide steps during jumping-in situations. By changing the toddler on the floor on soft mats, wearing swimming shoes, and making jumping-in situations safe with the use of soft mats, these dangers can be prevented. Shoulder, head, elbow or wrist injuries such as grazing, straining or cuts can occur in jumping-in situations when the parents keep an unsuitably safe distance to their child, resulting in him landing directly on them instead of in the water. Water's resistance prevents them from drifting back again. The danger with the first jumping attempts—falling into the water from a sitting position at the edge of the pool—is that the toddler can scrape his head or back off the edge when he doesn't lean forward enough. Hand, elbow or shoulder injuries can occur when the child is held the wrong way, e.g. when the parents, instead of holding his trunk, place their hands out; then when he falls, they push him back up again with their hands to prevent him from going under. This is why a course instructor must explain the different *grip techniques* beforehand in detail, so that the parents can carry them out in practice, being corrected where necessary.

◆ *Poisoning* can occur when a child drinks large amounts of chlorinized water, shower gel /shampoos or foot disinfectant. By supporting the child's head securely above water, and keeping an eye on him (in the shower rooms, as well) this can be avoided. Pool water is of drinking water standard, i.e. sipping this alone does not cause poisoning (water intoxication).

◆ *Bouts of suffocation* can occur when small objects go down the wrong way. They enter the airways and partially or completely block the lungs. Therefore, both course instructor and parents must always examine playing material. To avoid a sudden fall or a tumble into the water, where the child's head is underwater for a while, and he starts gasping for air and panicking, an accompanying adult must be *within reaching distance* at all times. Toddlers have to be made familiar with the safety rules and signals (see chapter 1.3 "Safety training"), i.e. they are only allowed to sit or stand on the steps, or the edge when a parent is in the water, and has given a signal to jump. Danger is lurking when parents aren't watching for a second, and the children swim out of their parents' reach with a swimming ring or water wings. (A comment here: older brothers or sisters can only be integrated into the course to a limited extent for this reason; a second accompanying person is recommended. Because of the lack of supervision, one cannot allow the older child to swim around on his own with swimming aids or stand waiting at the edge of the pool. Experience shows that parents are inclined to widen their distance to the child when swimming aids are used, as they assume their child to be in safety.)

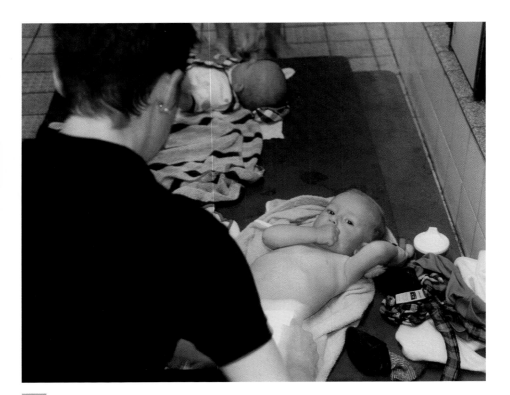

Methodical Procedure when Something Has Gone Down the Wrong Way

When something has been swallowed the wrong way (aspiration) e.g. small hard pieces, it is necessary to get the child to cough. In the case of solid objects, one lays the child stomach down on one's thighs and slaps him on the back 3 to 4 times, or the child is lying flat, and is being held at the shoulder and hip joints, and is then suddenly turned almost upside-down, back and forth, giving the object the opportunity to move up and out of the baby's airways. If the child swallows water the wrong way, coughing and sneezing set in on reflex, thus transporting the water back out again. By holding the child close to one's body, with eye contact, calming words of affection, and by supporting the back of his head, as well as tapping his back, his condition is usually brought back to normal quickly.

One differentiates between "wet" and "dry" drowning. *Dry drowning* (10% of cases) is associated with an epiglottal cramp, i.e. because of the water which has entered the mouth or throat the epiglottis pushes itself in front of the trachea to prevent water from getting into the lungs. If the child is rescued in time, artificial breathing is usually enough for successful resuscitation.

In the case of wet *drowning* (90% of cases), the child is not found immediately. Through exhaustion the epiglottis relaxes again so that water gets into the lung, and therefore, into the blood circulation which can lead to life-threatening disruption of heart and kidney functions. A description exists of a successful resuscitation in freshwater even with children who were under water for 20 minutes or longer. Saltwater drowning is much more dangerous, and a child can only survive with intensive medical treatment.

Methodical Steps when a Child Seems to Have Stopped Breathing/ Drowning Situation

Quick action is needed here and all measures must be taken immediately. Drowning is when a child loses consciousness; if he stops breathing, or it comes to cardiovascular standstill, medical assistance must be sought immediately. When a child is still breathing, he must be immediately laid down on the floor in a lateral position wrapped up warm and dry and then comforted.

If after brief observation (nostril or chest movements), and attempts at stimulation (talking to him, blowing, shaking), a child is found to be not breathing, one must clear his mouth, slightly overstretch his head (not as far as with an adult), then close his mouth by pressing under the chin (the other hand holds the back of his head), and immediately begin with artificial breathing of the nose four times (*mouth-to-nose resuscitation*). After this one must look and see if the child comes around again, and continues breathing spontaneously.

If after having checked the pulse rate on his upper arm, the child is still not breathing, one continues with artificial breathing at a rate of *30 breaths per minute* until the paramedics arrive or the child begins breathing again on his own, i.e. 1x every two seconds with a breathing volume of 100-150ml per breath (check pulse every minute).

Methodical Steps in the Case of Cardiovascular Failure

When neither breathing nor pulse is evident, then the heart has stopped beating. In this case, artificial breathing must be carried out in sequence with cardiac massage on a hard surface. The right place to press when doing cardiac massage is on the lower half of the breastbone (skightly left), i.e. under an imaginary line of connection between the nipples. The index, middle and ring finger are placed here, and the chest is pushed down vertically by about 2.5—4cm *fifteen times in close succession*.

There should be three compressions in two seconds (approx. 80 presses per minute).

The working cycle of *three breathing processes in alternation with fifteen cardiac massages* is to be continued until the paramedics arrive, or the child has been reanimated. If the heart begins to beat again, i.e.one can feel a pulse rate, then only breathing should be continued.

Comment: It's generally hard to feel a toddler's pulse rate (hand, groin and throat arteries); a strong grip of the upper am is, therefore, recommended, which parets can practice while bathing.

The general rule is: in the case of an accident, the course instructor must act in a deliberate way, above all stay calm and not lose his head! The tasks must be divided up in order for the rescue chain to work, i.e. one person informs the rescue service (emergency telephone number) with details on the accident (place, number and age of persons involved and type of accident), another carries out the first aid procedures, another holds towels, mat etc.

For the person doing the breathing, it is very important that he takes deep breaths himself, so as to prevent circulation problems. In order to find the right working rhythm for artificial breathing, a "training period" of 1-2 minutes is necessary.

6 Course Contents and Practice

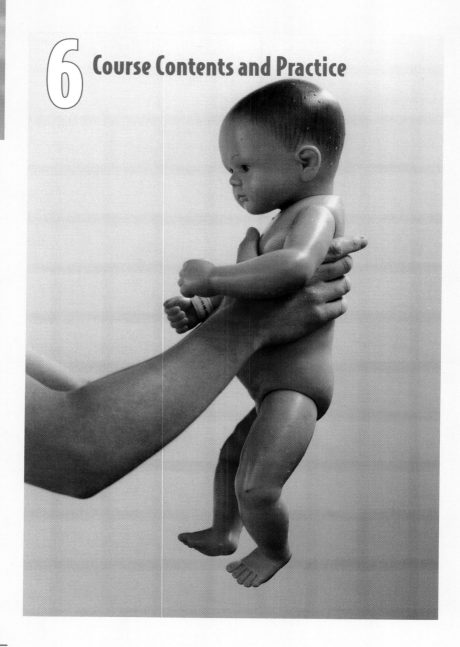

6.1   Run of Events and Contents of a Course

Particularly in his second year of life, a toddler's day-to-day form, concentration and emotional stability are subject to considerable fluctuation. Parents occasionally think that their child is no longer interested in swimming, or that he never was interested in the first place. However, the development of a child's ego, the conflict inside him as he proceeds to gain more independence, are factors that also leave their mark while swimming. This is particularly noticeable when the child has missed out on some lessons, e.g. because of illness, and he then has to learn to get accustomed to the situation again; a phase which generally passes after a few weeks.

It often helps here to cope with the child's problems patiently on one hand, and on the other hand, give him a supportive routine for orientation, i.e. going to lessons regularly and punctually while always being aware of how to help the child with compromises and time-outs in a bid to encourage his positive reaction.

Toddlers receive *integral motivation*[16] which encourages them to open up more and more. The first priority with beginners is to get the child feeling comfortable in water and not to overtax him. Within the group that he gets to know, he orients himself to his surroundings, becomes familiar with the run of events, and strikes up contacts with others. The first few lessons run relatively smoothly; the course instructor explains his ideas and their purpose, and offers asistance when difficulties arise, or when the child is having problems adapting.

The initial unsureness among the children and parents, and reserved communication among the group members soon disappears when a certain routine has set in. At the end of the first course, one can generally identify progress in water accustomization: the child is more confident and familiar with the situation, the other people and with the water. In a follow-up course, the lessons continue to build on everything the child already knows as the lessons are adapted to the child's age and development phase.

---

[16] Learning opportunities which aid personality development, i.e. by encouraging both the physical motor abilities and the social, emotional and intellectual abilities, as well as sensitising perception.

Those reactions learned in baby swimming are consolidated through repetition on the one hand, and on the other hand, the exercises are varied, so that the children learn to react more fluently and flexibly. Tasks are combined, put in order, put together and linked, so as to extend and complete little action processes.

There are four methodical didactic principles to be brought into effect when organizing a lesson: the lesson should promote the toddler *integrally, healthily, and at a level appropriate to his development*, and one should work *in pleasant harmony with the water*. Lesson content should be didactically structured in such a way that the tasks always move from easy to *difficult and from simple to complex*, both in their methodical procedure and time duration. The idea is to encourage parent-child play in the water to such an extent that it becomes an adventure, and learning experience for both parties concerned.

For toddlers aged one-and-a-half (beginners), the course can be thematically structured according to the following pattern:

Lesson and main theme focus

1st lesson: getting used to the swimming pool, group and course instructor (group)

2nd lesson: discovering the water and its properties (water)

3rd lesson: getting to know each other and becoming used to water in one's face (accustomizing to water)

4th lesson: developing and testing strength (strength)

5th lesson: getting to know one's body, and its movement capacity (flexibility)

6th lesson: showing endurance and controlling breath (diving)

7th lesson: moving forward with parents' help and/or swim wings (safety training and locomotion)

8th lesson: climbing, jumping, hanging —elementary forms of movement (motor skills)

9th lesson: music—making music in the pool (perception and creative play)

10th lesson: learning with and from others (skillfulness, child swapping)

Equipment/materials and forms of play

◆ mats for tunnel games
◆ building bricks of different color to collect, swap and sort

◆ hose at inflow (bubbles, fountain)
◆ big and small watering cans, funnels (river)
◆ beakers or bowls (pouring)
◆ swimming pool on mats (lake)
◆ baskets as boats (surrounded by swimming tubes)

◆ group activities and imitation tasks with water animals, bowls for water accustomization (water-pouring method)
◆ doll as a model

◆ parent-child sports with skillfulness tasks, and activities using swimming boards or rubber hoses at the edge for strengthening purposes.

◆ gymnastic games to promote body perception using pot scrubbers, sponges, lines and cloths

◆ beach balls for kicking, catching, throwing.
◆ frisbees and blowpipes

◆ fetching, bringing and sorting activities at the edge with swim wings as equipment first, and then later as buoyancy aid on upper arm

◆ jumping games from parent's body, from quadro diving platform, from the edge of the pool with climbing tasks over mats and obstacles, crooked surfaces.

◆ singing, sound and noise activities, tasks with bells, pipes, bottles, rattles, keys, cassette recorder

◆ throwing different types of balls through hoops
◆ target and distance throwing with game partners and child swapping

If we look back at chapter 5.1 in regards to planning lesson content, and then look at this sample structure, it becomes clear that the lesson structure is not determined by strict goal achievement, but rather is filled with elements of variety and creativity. Each lesson does have the same systematic structure, but is based on different contents, and this is what gives it its variable and creative structure. Starting out with getting the children accustomized to the water, one then moves on to *basic swimming skills* (gliding, breathing out in water, diving, jumping, moving forward), and each child continues working on perfecting these skills at his own individual level. Thus, one constantly takes new approaches to lesson elements, assigning different levels of intensity to them from lesson to lesson.

6.2   Constructing a Lesson, Lesson Content and Creative Structure of a Lesson

The magical 4 (from the methodical didactic principles) appear again for structuring each lesson—but this time in the form of phases:

◆ In the first phase (approx. 5 minutes), the child is *acclimatizing* himself to the surroundings, and to the water covering his body; his cardiovascular sytem is activated. The parent has close body contact to the child, and walks around the pool with him, massaging his body and caressing his head with water. Gradually the parents intensify their movements while walking and hopping, and then take their child out of this close skin and body contact position, and place him in the "face-to-face" grip, so as to consciously have eye contact with him. During this exercise, the child's circulation is further activated by raising and lowering his body.

◆ In the second phase (approx. 5 minutes), the toddler's legs are stimulated through caressing and shaking, so that he can *perceive them more consciously*. Through swaying, pushing and pulling movements in all directions against the water resistance the child's sensations of skin, movement and position are sensitized, and his orientative capacity is challenged at the same time. These new movements have the further aim of regulating muscle tone, and making the joints more flexible.

◆ In the third phase (approx. 15 minutes), the child is increasingly encouraged *to move himself*. With the minimal amount of parental support required (hand under the chest), he is motivated to act and react with his limbs thanks to water splashes, currents and touching impulses on the soles of his feet, or brief passive limb movements (guided splashing of the hands on the water surface).

With the help of splashing games and the water-pouring test[17], the child's willingness to dive under can be assessed, as well as his mouth-closing

---

[17] The water pouring test examines the emitional attitude of a child towards water. Trust to this medium is built step by step using streaming water, not splashing.

and non-breathing reflexes. Only when he accepts water in his face, holds his breath under control, and he indicates a cognitive willingess (anticipation) can a brief dive be initiated, step by step for 1-2 seconds. The child is challenged to show positioning reflexes, and balancing reactions to flying, falling, grasping, supporting and turning movements; he learns to react appropriately. The retaining and motion muscles are strengthened through continual play activities; the child's mobility is universally challenged and promoted.

◆ In the fourth phase (approx. 5 min), the child should be able or enabled to *relax* and satisfy his urge to play and discover. The child can pursue his interests without any instructions, and should not be disturbed. Rocking cradle movements in supine position or a reclined sitting position calm down the baby's respiratory and cardiovascular systems, and the stimuli are gradually reduced toward the end of the lesson.

Examples of Lesson Content

Theme: Moving around with colored balls in various ways and with certain aims.

Apparatus: Basket with balls of a swimming line (red/white), large mats or styrodur floats.

Phase	Objective	Methodical content structure
1	greeting	◆ Frontal circle, CI in the middle: "Hello children, hello children, let's all wave hello, then come to me, then come to me, and now off we go." (P push T into the middle of the circle (3 times)
	group contact	◆ 1-2-3-in a jumble: P push T through the circle.
	stimulate circulation	"Turn-a, turn-a, turn a-round (P hold T in face-to-face position, and then turn him along his longtitudinal axis by throwing him up gently, ri/le)
	getting used to water	◆ Splashing hands, kicking feet, P sit their T side-saddled on their thighs and say "Splish and splash, the water flows, on my hair and on my nose, from my nose down to my toes, it stops a bit and makes no sound, then it splashes on the ground" (slap water with hand)
2	passive movement	◆ In a line 2-3m away from the edge of the pool: "I'm a little jumping jack, and I'm swimming/gliding/jumping to the edge and back -1-2-3 wheee!," P push/pull T
	balance stimulation	◆ T standing or sitting on P's hands (hand bowls), balancing the body, lose balance in between and then P hold them again as far as the edge (taxi game)

Toddler Swimming

Phase	Objective	Methodical content structure
3	activate the children to move by themselves	◆ gliding/moving forward: get balls on one side, and bring them to the other side (target throwing into the overflow, gliding towards the edge, moving forwards
		◆ functional game: let the balls roll down a board, and grasp them at the other side.
		◆ perception: sorting out the balls according to the color song: "red, red, red are the colors of etc. etc." (or looking for a color, and then gathering them).
		◆ hand skills: place the balls on top of each other (building a tower), or put them in a row on a mat in the middle, or at the edge
		◆ breathing: blowing and blubbering into the water through the hole in the balls, looking through the hole.
		◆ skillfulness: T are sitting on a mat and place the balls over the P's fingers.
		◆ jumping: T jump out of sitting position from the mats and take hold of the balls, which are on the P's fingers (perhaps with diving).
		◆ diving: P hold a ball in the water with outstretched arm, T try to see this ball underwater (perhaps by moving down arm, dipping and grasping).
		◆ jumping: T crawl/run across the mat route and jump off

Phase	Objective	Methodical content structure
4	Relaxation Finish up Saying goodbye	◆ body awareness: bedding oneself in balls, in sitting position collect as many balls as possible, tidy up and throw all but one into the basket. ◆ foot or body massage: roll the ball along the T's plantar arch. ◆ tidying up: give the rest of the balls in the basket to the CI ◆ goodbye song: "This is the way we say goodbye etc."

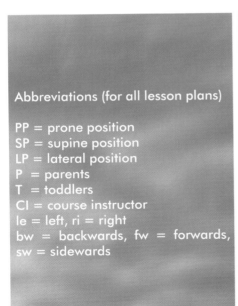

Abbreviations (for all lesson plans)

PP = prone position
SP = supine position
LP = lateral position
P = parents
T = toddlers
CI = course instructor
le = left, ri = right
bw = backwards, fw = forwards,
sw = sidewards

Theme: Body Perception

Equipment: Colored cloths, line and clothes pins, pool noodles

Phase	Objective	Methodical Content Structure
1	Greeting	◆ Frontal circle: CI stands in the middle and introduces all children by their names with a song:
	Stimulate circulation	"Hello, hello, how nice it is, how nice it is that you're here today. X is here and X is here, now we're all here, let's give a big cheer!"
	Group contact	◆ T in pairs opposite each other, verse: "Up and down, up and down we're always going up and down." Gradually increase speed, change partners
	Getting to know the room	◆ Tie washing line on one side, hold the other. Walking along the line, holding it and pulling it, going under it (Abracadabra -line goes up), trying to grasp it. Hanging cloths on the line: Line up high (raindrops), line down lower (washing one's face), hide-and-seek (peek-a-boo), slalom around the cloths.
2	Passive movement	◆ Making waves: T hold line, are pushed to and fro by P in trophy grip or T are rocking ("Show me your feet"; PP/SP) Line up high: P place themselves under the line and push/ pull / swing the T fw, bw, sw under the line (in face-to-face position).
		◆ The Line up: P get beneath the line and push/pull/swing their T through the line fw/sw/bw.

Toddler Swimming

Phase	Objective	Methodical Content Structure
3	Activate the children to move by themselves	◆ Water accustomizing/diving: T sitting on P shoulders, fall/fly towards the line, first sw, then diving in fw (first only splashes, then half of the face, then whole face), P do it first / together with T.
		◆ Movement and catching game: playing chase in pairs, one T has two cloths, the other tries to catch the tips.
		◆ Movement and upward grasping: P place the bundled cloth on top of head, P pull T behind them in PP, T try to pull the cloth down off P's head.
		◆ Strengthening: P hold cloth at each end; T standing on P's thighs, grasps cloth and hangs on it.
4	Relaxation Finish up Saying goodbye	◆ Perception: P hide their heads under cloth (Song: "I'm looking for my ....please tell me where they are? Ah they've come right back to me, tralalalalalala"), T go in hiding.
		◆ Sailing in a boat, rocking: tie two pool noodles together, the cloth is the floor is held together by clothes pins. "The ships in a row, rocking to, rocking fro, just lie down and close your eyes, soon it's time for beddy-byes"
		◆ Tidying up, goodbye song: "This is the way we say goodbye, say goodbye,....etc"

Theme: Water games at different stations

Equipment: Tubes/hoses (washing machine), drinking straws, beakers, basin/bath, watering cans, pipes, paddling pool, mats.

Phase	Objective	Methodical Content Structure
1	Greeting	◆ Song: "We want to say hello, and we do it like this: hello (splash, splash) hello (splash, splash). 3x
	Stimulate circulation	◆ T in embrace position with P Song: "Water is for washing up (3x), wash-ing up" (Variations: scooping, dripping, splashing, paddling, kicking).
2	Passive movement	◆ Frontal circle, swinging: pulling the T sw, fw/bw through the water in rhythm with "Wa-ter wa-ving." ◆ Frontal circle: T sitting on P's thighs: "Ride a little horsey, ride to town; Ride a little horsey, but don't fall down, etc etc..," tilting ri/le, fw/bw, falling with a splash
	Perception Locomotion	◆ Stop moving game: T piggyback on P, P run around, T are kicking, and then come to a sudden stop.
3	Activate children's own movement Perception Play Fine motor activities	Station activities (two P-T pairs at each station: **1.** Water flows out (hose attached to inflow pipe like a fountain), T feels water with his hands and feet. **2.** Scoop water (from the pool onto mats), T is sitting scooping out water, P scooping it in.

Phase	Objective	Methodical Content Structure
		3. Water drops: Perforated mat as tunnel, with watering cans pour water over P-T pair when crossing tunnel. **4.** Water flows as lubricant: a T pours water onto the slide (float), the other T slides. **5.** Water bubbles: blow bubbles in the water with straws. **6.** Cold and warm water: fill a basin with cold water and climb in/place hands inside. **7.** Water is buoyant: sailing boats—climbing in, getting out, the other T pushes/pulls and kicks.
4	Relaxation Finish up Saying goodbye.	◆ Water massage in reclined sitting position, head leaning on P shoulder (Relax): shake out legs/arms/body underwater, moisten body with water. ◆ Goodbye song: "This is the way......"

6.2.1   Basic Movement Forms and Basic Skills in Water

Learning to swim is a procedure which occurs step by step, according to the teaching principles of *water accustomization, water management and locomotion*. The child develops basic skills and *competence* by actively dealing with water. Water should become a familiar medium of movement, in which he can experience himself, and his body, and develop his personality and relationship to other people.

Getting accustomed to the water and managing to cope with it are both factors that lay the foundation for the independent and endurant type of swimming movement later. If the child feels comfortable in the water and associates it with positive experiences and exciting challenges, he will continue to do this and move on to swimming of his own free will.

The key element of water *accustomization* refers to preparing for and relating to water's properties and characteristics, i.e.

◆ its liquid consistency.
◆ its varying temperatures.
◆ the pressure it exerts on chest and body.
◆ its buoyancy effects on the body (particularly the legs).
◆ its resistance force which hinders movement (due to its density).

There are numerous opportunities for this process to take place, e.g.

◆ relaxing showering rituals with watering cans, keys, bowls and shower hoses, while also varying the temperature.
◆ making waves in the swimming pool with hands and feet, letting water drizzle down, constructing dripstone caves and waterfalls and using it to splash, froth up, paddle and kick with.
◆ using vessels for filling, pouring, emptying and transporting water.

Toddlers learn to *cope with water* mainly by practicing basic swimming skills through physical experience, such as

◆ *floating* in prone and supine position either supported by the parents' hands or swimming aids.
◆ *breathing* out into the water.

◆ *jumping* into the water.
◆ *gliding* toward the edge of the pool in prone position (having been given a push by his parents), and then holding on.
◆ *dipping* the head into the water after flying, sliding, jumping.

Moving around in the water initially means the transferral of familiar movement possibilities from dry land onto water situations. Thus, toddlers are carried and moved through the water to music, to songs or to poems. This introduction promotes their coordination and orientation capacities. This includes:

◆ varying the *type of movement* (e.g. walking, running, hopping, galloping, twisting, jumping, turning, swimming).
◆ changing the *direction of movement*,i.e. forwards, backwards, sideways, as well as upwards and downwards.
◆ varying the *rhythm of movement* (slowing down, quickening up, stopping in between, e.g. fast-slow).
◆ changing the *movement dynamics* (e.g. gentle, rough).
◆ having an organized structure in the *movement tasks* (e.g. in pairs, small groups, station work).
◆ changing the *group formation* (e.g.circle, square, snake form, passage).

Orientation guides and materials can be helpful in the lesson e.g. clothes lines, ropes, cordoning tape, mat tunnels, traffic cones or boards at, above, or on the edge of the pool. Large canisters of water or suction cups can be used to hold clothes lines, particularly when the edge of the pool is at the same height as the water.

In the second year of life, the toddler begins with initial, arbitrary attempts to move forward. In certain stimulative situations, he sets his own targets, choosing the movement direction by himself in the process. His parents must expect this, and be prepared for it with flexible grip techniques and by changing hands. If the children are using swimming aids, they are by no means capable of moving forward effectively over long distances with their short, kicking limbs, and the huge amount of effort involved. They can manage only a few meters at the most. In the third year of life, these forward movements become more relevant. Toddlers like to dip their head into the water occasionally. Remarkably enough they are already capable of swimming forward under water in prone position for 2-3m without any help, the leg- kicking movements alone driving them ahead.

Toddlers can be animated to expand this initial form of movement over a certain distance by *dog paddling*[18] with the arms:

◆ Jumping from the edge, diving platform (built from the quadro system) or mat, and then moving forwards towards the parents (recommendation: head-first slow drop into the water from sitting position, jump from standing position).
◆ Forward movement toward the edge from a sitting position on parent's shoulder or standing position on parent's hands/thighs.
◆ Forward movement to the edge on a swimming board from sitting/standing position.
◆ Being pushed backwards to the edge in prone position; moving towards parents by kicking legs and feet (reverse parking).
◆ Hand over hand movement around the corner from one edge to the other (crossing the corner).
◆ Jumping, gliding, moving to and fro between two persons.
◆ Jumping or gliding mat to mat from a sitting position (island hopping, tie perforated mats to the mat route with gaps in between, and then hoist up from one edge to the other).

[18] Compact hitting and pulling strokes of each arm in alternation underneath the chest area, an elementary form of the crawl.

Toddlers cannot actively jump or push themselves off, but let themselves fall into the water initially. To prevent injuries, they must be given support assistance here, and perhaps a little shove in the back or posterior. It is important that the children become aware of their legs: when sitting with their back to their parent, they are able to see their legs and how they move, which in turn triggers off feedback of the motor and nervous systems. Guiding the children's legs, stroking the front and back of their legs, as well as touching the insteps or soles of their feet can all help the development of effective leg work. The child also registers the feeling and observation of his parents' leg movements[19], and how he is moved along with these movements, and this encourages the child even more.

---

[19] Parents hang at the edge in supine position, kicking their legs. The child sits on his parent's stomach facing outwards. This exercise can also be carried out with pool noodle rings.

6.2.2   Gymnastic Exercises and Climbing About on a Parent in the Water

Carrying out the following exercises in water with melodic voice accompaniment can make shoulder joints, spinal column and hip joints more elastic and supple in the second and third year of life.

◆ "How big are you? Sooo big."
The child sits on his parent's raised thigh facing out to the front; the water is up to his chest. He holds on to his parent's hands as they lift their arms from the side up into the air.

◆ "How much do you love yourself? Sooo much."
The child sits as above holding onto his parent's hands who then crosses his arms.

◆ "All feet up high in the air!"
The child is lying in the relax grip, his head leaning on his parent's shoulder.The adult's hands are around the child's calves, and after "Up" pull them up towards the shoulders, thus causing a rolling movement of the spine. The spine can be stretched by placing a hand under the child's back and "All tummies up high in the air."

◆ Hands-a-clapping tap, tap, tap, and now the legs tap, tap, tap":
The child is held in the relax grip, his head leaning on his parent's shoulder. The parent's hands are around the child's calves, opening and closing his legs.

◆ "Click-click-clack, the legs bend back."
The child lies as above, his parents holding his calves; they then push each knee towards his stomach in alternation, the other leg is then outstretched (also possible with both legs at the same time).

The following climbing and skillfulness activities are suitable for strengthening and burning off energy:

◆ Mountain climbing:
The child is standing on his parent's thighs and is holding on to his hands; he then climbs over leg, abdomen and chest up to the

shoulders. On "1-2-3" the child climbs down again or is tilted over. This exercise can also be done on the parent's back, finishing off with a jump to the front.

◆ Washing your hair:
The child is sitting on the adult's abdomen or chest (or piggy-back), his feet are around the stomach or neck. Now the child should lie down, dip his hair in the water, and then swing up again. The lumbar spine is to be supported here (this exercise is generally only accepted by children in their third year of life).

◆ Keeping your balance:
The child is standing on the adult's hands, facing out to the front. At the beginning he is up to his belly-button in water, later he is in a higher position. This exercise can be intensified by supporting only one leg at a time.

◆ Shoulder handstand:
The child is facing his parent, supporting himself on his shoulder. He is then held up with support of the stomach/pelvis area, so that he ends up in a handstand position,.

◆ Trophy and flickknife:
The child is held in the trophy grip. He has his feet set in support at his parent's stomach/pelvic area, and then tenses up his whole body. When relaxing his back muscles, he rolls back up again etc.

◆ Head flight:
The child climbs onto his parent's back holding his hands, and lies stomach-down on his head. Then he stretches his entire body to an aeroplane, and can be turned.

6.2.3   Grip Techniques with Ideas for Games and Exercises

Due to his swimming age (3-12 months), a baby is unable to hold up his head and body steadily, or keep them in balance. Because of this and particularly because of the fact that young (for the first time) parents still require practice in safe handling, the Grip ABC that is taught in these courses offers assistance and, indeed, represents a major part of each lesson. A toddler, on the other hand, has developed his strengths to such an extent that he can bring himself into upright position, and he now wishes to change his position and direction of movement as he pleases.

Having learned to stay upright, the child generally prefers to have his body in vertical position in the water, too. This is particularly noticeable when the child pushes himself away from his parent's lower arms, and tries to upright himself out of prone position. Grip positions with children in the second year of life should, therefore, be varied to enable the child to assume a vertical position of the body (standing in the water). Several sample activities can be found at the end of this section. Balancing abilities at this age are still not fully developed, however, causing him to lose confidence in his movements in the water, too— reinforced through buoyancy force—and become clingy.

A child of this age generally refuses supine position as his radius of perception and grasping activities are limited in supine position. This position is perceived as unpleasant and uncontrollable. In his third year of life, a toddler becomes very active in the water. His splashing and kicking is much stronger, and he is tempted to move around. He prefers swimming on his stomach (at approx. 45°), is often almost in a horizontal position when gliding or dipping his head in the water, and is capable of movement of high endurance in this position.

The child's head should be clearly above the water surface (stops water swallowing) without him having to overstretch himself (no wrinkles across his back, his feet in the water). Slight pressure on his bottom helps to stop this overstretched position, and the legs go back into the water. In quiet moments, he voluntarily assumes supine position again. He is not used to having his ears in the water making him fight it now and then. Nevertheless, he should be encouraged to take on a flat gliding position.

One must generally ensure that the children are supported at the breastbone (centre of mass), and can move their arms and legs freely. As non-swimmers, they should feel safe and contented in their parents' hands, so that they can research and discover the adventures of water more or less without limits, without feeling afraid, and with full curiosity.

The grip should be tight enough for the child to feel *held*, however, not so tight that his body, scope of movement and action (particularly in the shoulder area) is restricted. The water's buoyancy eases the muscular support given by the parents, so that they can limit this support to being a safety function only. It is merely the child's insufficient strengths of buoyancy and locomotion which are to be supported by the parents' hands.

Parents should ensure that
◆ they are up to their shoulders in water.
◆ they are always at eye level with their children.
◆ they keep a constant eye on their child's chin, so that the child does not swallow any water.
◆ they regularly moisten those body parts which are not in the water, so as to prevent them from cooling.
◆ the child does not have to overstretch himself when held in prone position (no wrinkles across his back, feet in the water, perhaps slight pressure on the bottom).
◆ they choose the direction the child is facing for movement in the water (e.g. when collecting equipment).

Listed below are several grips from the Grip ABC from the book *Baby Swimming*, which I have updated with illustrations, as well as further ideas for games and exercises.

Ideas for games and exercises

◆ Water bows: Moving through the water and turning (to the right, to the left).

◆ Give me five: Running through the water, and greeting other course participants by slapping their hand. Parents demonstrate, children follow suit.

◆ Dancing time: The child holds on with one hand behind his back, the other hand ready in dance position. Then, gallop through the water in polka rhythm (hip support on the left and right in alternation).

◆ Washing hair: The child sits on the adult's abdomen, and is told to lean back. His back is supported and his hair is being washed, drifting to the right and to the left.

◆ Kangaroo: The child sits on the adult's abdomen, and is told to hold on tightly.

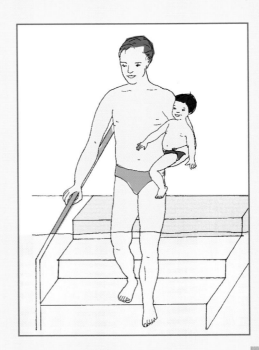

Figure 1:
Single-handed carrying grip at the side—straddle.

Ideas for games and exercises

◆ Water waves: the child is pulled forward and backward against the water's resistance, changing the movement tempo, and with rhythmical verse accompaniment.

◆ Having a snack: "I'm hungry........and I'm going to nibble your right shoulder." The parents encourage the child to laugh by nibbling various parts of his body.

◆ See-saw: "I am big and you are big, I am gone—and you are still there. Hooray! Parents go up high, the children are lifted up, the parents dip into the water and come back up again.

◆ Movement verse: "Turning, turning, round and round, jumping, jumping, up and down, flying, flying through the air, landing, landing, now we're there." Parents turn, jump, lift the children; they start off quickly, and gradually reduce speed until they stop completely. Slow down spoken rhythm as appropriate.

◆ Footwork: "Feet to the front, feet to the back, to the right and to the left, kicking here and kicking there till they come up in the air, flying high up in the sky, and here they stay both high and dry!" Parents swing their children in different directions and finally lift them up out of the water, so that they end up lying on their parent's head.

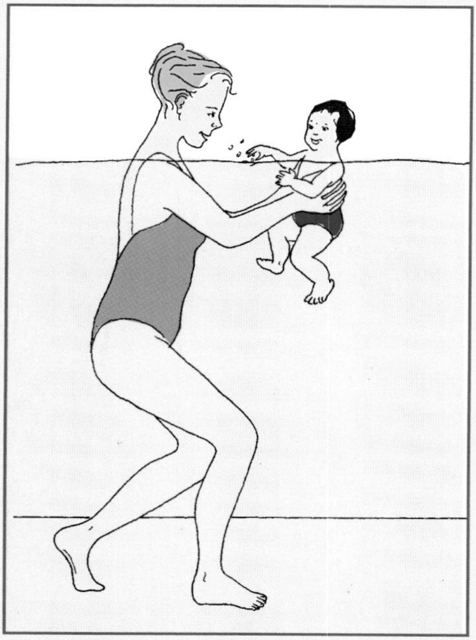

Figure 2:
Double-handed frontal waist-grip with child in vertical position—face to face

Ideas for games and exercises

◆ Driving: The parents run backwards pulling the children along. The drive becomes an active adventure with slalom rides, beeping and buzzing noises, push and pull movements and stops.

◆ Stamping concert: The parents stand in a line near the edge of the pool holding their children in the water. The course instructor holds onto the edge in prone position and stamps his feet with different intensities. The children should imitate this.

◆ Blubber bubble concert: The parents blubber into the water in front of their children, and try to produce various vocal tones. The children are encouraged to imitate.

◆ Head shaking: The parents dip their head in the water, and then shake it out again. The children imitate this.

◆ Water tasting: The parents stand in the water at the edge, sip some water and spit it out again into the overflow. The children imitate this.

Figure 3:
Double-handed frontal grip in prone position + shoulders secured: chalice

Note:
Due to the child's weight and his desire to remain upright in the water, this grip is seldom used with children in the second and third years of life. Place the palms of the hands together under the child's chest with the fingers out to his sides, supporting his chest from below, so as not to overstrain the wrists.

Ideas for games and exercises

◆ Wave drive: The parents walk backwards, pulling their children in waves. These wave movements can be up and down, back and forth, lurch from side to side or totally irregular.

◆ Weight lifting: The parents dive in underneath their child, and then lift him up step by step.

◆ Holding on: The parents walk backwards, pulling their children alongside the edge of the pool, turning towards and against the wall in alternation. They encourage their child to react quickly and grasp the wall when approaching it, and then pull himself inwards. Movement direction is also changed.

◆ Flying balance: The parents run backwards, and tilt their children to the left and to the right.

◆ Stranded: The parents go under the water, and push the children towards a mat which they can then hold onto.

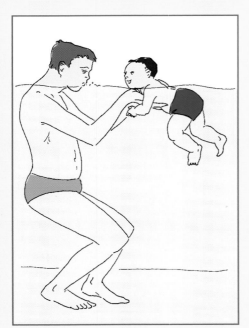

Figure 4:
Double-handed frontal grip in prone position without shoulder support—basket

Ideas for games and exercises

◆ Test of strength: The children hold onto their parents' thumbs. While they gradually lift their children up slightly out of the water, they count out loud to see how long the children can hold on.

◆ Pendulum: The children are pulled through the water to the left and right.

◆ One-arm hang: The children are told to let go of one arm (in alternation).

◆ Stand up: The children are told to lie on their back, and with their heads resting on the water (sleeping). The parents push them along, and on the alarm call "Wake up and drive!" the children have to upright themselves, and kick strongly with their legs. Then, the parents walk backwards pulling them along.

◆ Walking up the wall: The parents stand in a line facing the edge, a distance of a child's legs away from the wall. The children are hanging on their parents' hands, and try to climb up the wall with their feet.

Figure 5:
Double-handed frontal thumb
grip—hanging swing

Note:

In order to cope with the children's changing body weight, the parents can make this exercise easier by dipping their shoulders right down into the water.

Ideas for games and exercises

◆ Staying upright: The parents move forwards and backwards; the children constantly try to regain their upright position.

◆ Diving: The parents stand near the edge of the pool. The children dive down out of the arm ring towards the wall.

◆ Hand over hand: The parents tell their children to move hand over hand along their arm, up as far as the neck, or around their whole body

◆ Showing direction: The children determine the direction of movement by pointing either to the left or right with their hands.

◆ Back swimming: The children are told to get into supine position, and kick their legs; the parents walk backwards in the process.

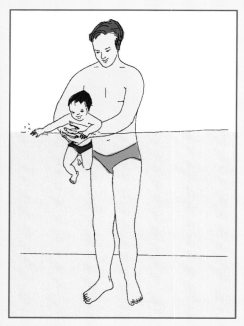

Figure 6:
Double-handed backward carrying grip under the arms: arm ring

Note:

This grip is very popular among toddlers in their second and third years of life. The children really enjoy being able to move arms and legs freely with a clear view ahead.

Ideas for games and exercises

◆ Looking for someone: The course instructor gets all particpiants to move around the pool. On a *clapping signal* he asks:"Where is ....?" All other children stop, look for the child in question, and move towards this child saying "There is..."

◆ Looking for the course instructor: Children and parents should close their eyes for a moment. Then, the course instructor dives under, moving around in the pool, and everyone looks for him, and then moves towards him. The course instructor comes back up again gradually.

◆ Push club: All participants stand behind each other—child-parent-child etc in a row. The children push the shoulders of the parent in front, who in turn offers slight resistance. The pair at the front change to the back after a while so as to be able to push, too.

◆ Sponge above the line: A line is spread out across the pool. The children throw sponges over this line from both sides. Those sponges which have landed in their area are picked up, and thrown over again.

◆ Fishing: Small plastic fish are in a basin. The course instructor pulls this basin to and fro across the whole pool, the children try and get a fish out.

Figure 7:
Double-handed backward waist grip with the child in diagonal position—trophy

Note:
Instead of using two adults, it is possible to do this exercise with toddlers by using the edge of the pool for holding on to.

Ideas for games and exercises

◆ Run-up: One parent holds the child at the waist, pushing and pulling him on the spot: Counting "1-2-3" the child is moved forwards and backwards, and then pushed over to the person opposite/to the edge of the pool.

◆ Butterfly: The children receive two boards and place each arm over a board. Giving little shoves at the waist or feet, the parents push the child over one length. Accompany this with "Butterfly" in melodic rhythm.

◆ Dolphin: The parents grasp their children around the waist, lift up one hand widely out of the water, and then let them dive under head first before gliding towards the edge of the pool underwater.

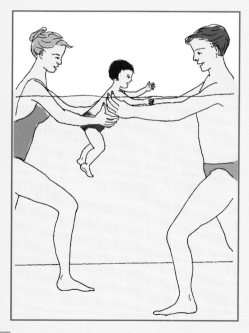

◆ Landing platform: The adult opposite shows his rounded back, so that the child can be pushed up his back, and then hold onto his shoulders.

◆ Long arms: The adult opposite turns sideways outstretching one arm over the water. The other person pushes the child towards this arm, so that the child can then be embraced, and pulled towards the body.

Figure 8:
Double-handed backward waist grip and a double-handed frontal underarm grip: hydroplane

Ideas for games and exercises

◆ Stiff as a board: The parents grasp the children by the elbow and hold them up. The children have to keep up body tension.

◆ Riding the waves: The children sit on the parents' hand bowls. The course instructor tells a vivid story showing how calm or rough the sea is.

◆ Tray: The children stand on their parents' hands (facing outwards) and are balanced by the water in high, low and sideward movements.

◆ Jumping jack: The children are standing on the parents' hands. The parents move their hands apart and back together again saying "I'm a little jumping jack, I move my legs out and move them back."

◆ One-legged stand: The children are told to stand on one leg on the hand bowls (in alternation) and try to balance.

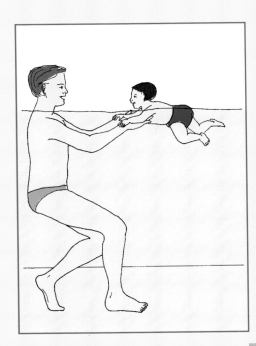

Figure 9:
Double-handed support grip
of the child's elbows/ hands/
posterior/ feet: hand bowls

Ideas for games and exercises

◆ Mountain train: Raising and lowering of the carrying arm.
◆ Tickling game with verse: "Round and round the garden." Fingers run up the arm up as far as the child's neck.
◆ Two-fingered back massage: With index and middle finger either side of the spine, the spinal column is massaged from the coccyx up to the neck.
◆ Push: Parent-child pairs run around in the pool and try to give the back of another pair a little push.
◆ Hand grabbing: The parent's free hand tries to grab other parents in front of the child's eyes. The child should grasp this game, trying it out with his own parents first, and then repeating it with other parents and children.

Figure 10:
Single-handed backward grip in prie position with the lower arm between the child's legs—leg tunnel

Ideas for games and exercises

◆ Touching the wall: The parents push their children towards the edge of the pool, and tell them to touch the wall with their hands and feet in alternation.

◆ Shake a leg: The parents grasp their child's left or right lower leg in alternation, and give it a good shake. After that the child is told to start kicking.

◆ Airplane: The parents grasp their child between the legs with one hand and support his chest with the other hand. They lift up their child in the air, and let it land with a splash on the water surface. This exercise prepares the child for conscious, headfirst diving.

◆ Big and small waves: The child is moved around on the water's surface in waves. When the course instructor calls out "Big waves", the children are lifted up into the air, and then land again as in the exercise above (airplane).

◆ Ejection seat: The child sits on his parent's hand (*hand bowls*) and—with the support of the other hand—is prepared for a fall into prone position through rocking movements backwards and forwards, until he tilts over.

Figure 11:
Single-handed lateral grip in prone position with a stabilising hand on the shoulders—sandwich

Ideas for games and exercises

◆ Washing hands: The parents sit their child onto their raised thigh, take hold of both arms, and rub their hands together. The child is thus encouraged to continue this movement by himself. Verse: "This is the way we wash our hands, wash our hands etc...." (The same can be done with slapping, splashing etc).

◆ Change of weather: The course instructor tells a story containing many dynamic elements e.g. sun, rain and storm. The parents and children do movements to these.

◆ Water is wet: Moisten different parts of the body with water singing "Water makes our body wet, body wet, body wet, water makes our body wet, body wet." (The same can be done with shoulder, legs, head).

◆ Big arms, small arms: The child is sitting on his parent's raised thigh, facing out to the front. The parents take hold of their child's lower arms and swing them forwards in circular movements (windmill). They then vary this exercise with shorter, quicker arm movements, so that they spoon up water: An accompanying verse could be: "Big arms pull and crawl, little arms spoon it all and tiny arms go splash, splash, splash."

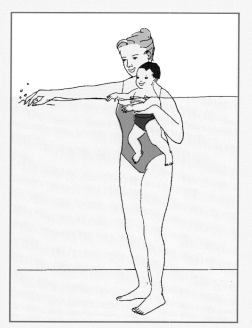

Figure 12:
Single-handed backward chest grip in vertical position—embrace

Ideas for games and exercises

◆ See-saw: The children lie stretched out with their stomachs on the parent's shoulder; the child's head is looking out over the back. The parents raise and lower the child's legs, so that he has to make compensatory movements.

◆ Frog leaps: Starting position as above. The parents take hold of their child's lower legs and guide them: pulling them in, straddling and then back together again. Accompany this movement with "Ribbit!"

◆ Kicking movements: Starting position as above. Parents take hold of their child's thighs with both hands and move his legs up and down in alternation (kicking movement). Take a break in between where the child can decide to continue the movement by himself—after initial encouragement.

◆ Shaking legs step by step: The parents take hold of one of the child's lower legs with both hands and loosen up his ankle by shaking slightly. Then the thigh is grasped and the knee joint is loosened in the same way. Now the child's waist is taken hold of as his whole leg up as far as his pelvis is raised and lowered. The same exercise is then repeated with the other leg.

◆ Shoulder handstand: The child supports himself with the hands on his parent's shoulders. He is then lifted up by his legs into handstand position.

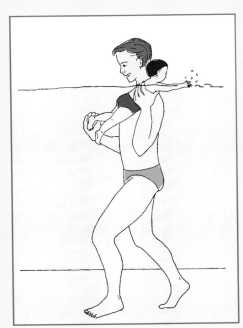

Figure 13:
Single-handed frontal prone position of the child leaning on the shoulders shoulder balance

Ideas for games and exercises

◆ Merry-go-round: The parents lead the children around their own body at various speeds and sing a merry-go-round song.

◆ Back and forth: The parents lead their child around their own body, tilting him into supine position at the front and into prone position at the back, so that the child can sit up afterwards each time; he must then tense up his abdominal muscles. The open hand stabilizes the neck and shoulder areas.

◆ Big waves and small waves: The parents lead their child around their own body, their free arm lying under his hip. The up and down wave movements are intensified from very small to very large waves until the child ends up being lifted out of the water, and then let him sink down again. Accompany this with melodic verse.

◆ Rolling in an out: The parents roll their child in sideways towards their shoulder by bending the arm and stretching it again. Accompany this with "Far away, up close."

◆ Hello and goodbye: With their free hand the parents shake the child's hand facing them ("Hello") and then pet/crawl down his body as far as his feet which they then give a shake ("Goodbye"). (Change of sides).

Figure 14:
Single-handed sideward prone position grip with upper arm support—merry-go-round

Ideas for games and exercises

◆ Feet up high in the air: The child leans on his parent's shoulder, in sitting position. The parents take hold of his lower arms, drum his feet on the water ("Footsies- footsies"), and then lift them up into the air ("Fly-ing high"), so that the spinal column is rounded.

◆ Sleep and get up: The child is leaning on his parent's shoulder. The parents hold their child's thighs from below, and tell them to come into upright position, and remain in a steady sitting position.

◆ Measuring feet: Standing face-to-face with another parent-child pair, the soles of each child's feet are placed together and measured.

◆ Foot catching: Two parent-child pairs stand opposite each other, one pair moves forwards, the other backwards; the pair walking forwards try and catch the other child's feet. The pairs switch places.

◆ Big toe: The parents massage each of their child's toes individually and call out their name in turn (Big toe, little toe..)

Figure 15:
Single-handed backward supine position of the child, leaning his head on parent's shoulder relax cheek-to-cheek

Toddler Swimming

Ideas for games and exercises

◆ Blowing bellies: The parents hold their child in sitting position (the child's calves are leaning on their shoulders) and guide the child with both hands towards their face until they can blow on the child's abdomen.

◆ Swinging: Rock the child to the left and the right under permanent eye contact. Sing along: "Rocking to, rocking fro, this is how we like to go."

◆ Whispering: The parents whisper something into the child's ears (in alternation), offering him the opportunity to do the same. Children with advanced speech comprehension (at about the end of the third year of life) can be asked to repeat what they heard.

◆ Facial expression: The parents use their mouth to make various facial expressions. The child is encouraged to imitate these.

◆ Mouth sounds: The parents produce various sounds with their mouth, and again the children are encouraged to imitate them.

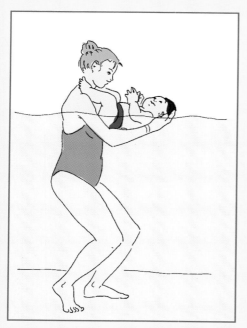

Figure 16:
Double-handed frontal supine position grip—head bowl vis-à-vis

Ideas for games and exercises

◆ Gliding towards the edge: The child sits on his parent's arm and glides toward the edge of the pool. A signal must be given here. When the child is experienced, and is prepared for water splashes, he can go underwater from a suitable distance, and then pull himself up at the edge.

◆ Lift: The child sits on his parent's hands. He is then raised slowly and told to jump off .His parents catch him again before he goes underwater. If the child is used to the water, he may dive underwater after jumping.

◆ High seat: The child sits on his parent's shoulders, his lower legs being held. He then is told to dive under (head first) a washing line with cloths or a tunnel.

◆ High stand: By holding on with the hands the child climbs up over his parent's back until he is standing on the shoulders; he then jumps down. *Important*: let go of the child's hands when he jumps.

◆ Hand support: Starting off in armchair position with support at the chest, the child is prepared for this exercise by leaning forward onto a mat and initiating/counting out loud the support movements. When the child has managed to support himself, he should then try, and climb onto the mat using his own strength.

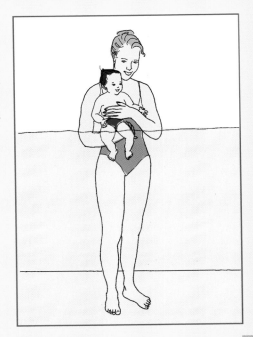

Figure 17:
Single-handed carrying grip with child in sitting position for jumps armchair

Toddler Swimming

Ideas for games and exercises

◆ Taxi: Climbing on and getting off the parent's back is practiced several times with the grips at the edge of the pool using the words: "Climb on" and "Climb off." The child is actively involved and motivated here by having to say where the taxi should drive to.

◆ Holding on, rodeo riding: The parents try and challenge their children to react to stop, start, twist and turn movements (holding on and keeping their balance).

◆ Tunnel ride: Parents and children enter various tunnel constructions throughout the pool—flat, high, narrow, wide etc. In the tunnels, vocal sounds are produced.

◆ Motor on, motor off: The parents stride through the pool; the children kick along for assistance. If the children stop kicking then the parents come to a halt.

◆ Going underwater together: First the parents walk under, e.g. a line with cloths. After that, they swim through the barrier. Finally, they dive under it. The child should be encouraged to imitate these movements. Counting out aloud helps the child.

Note:
Further grips for diving are dealt with in the next chapter.

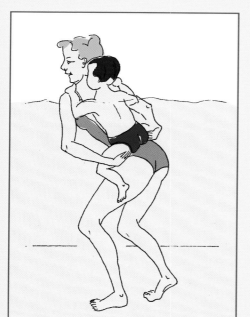

Figure 18:
Double-handed backward carrying grip on the adult's back with thigh stabilization rider

6.2.4   Getting Accustomed to Water and Diving Techniques

One of the main objectives of toddler swimming is getting the child accustomed to the water. The child should see his time in the water as relaxing, pleasant, educating and adventurous, and he should get to know the properties and effects of this element, learn to tolerate water on his own body, particularly on his head and face.

Water alters the body's position, as well as hearing, sight, smelling, tasting and breathing abilities. As soon as water runs over our face, we catch our breath (mouth-nose reflex). Nerves in our nose report a change in our breathing environment; breathing movement stops by reflex. The *larynx reflex* closes the *epiglottis* in the nose and throat area when we swallow to prevent the trachea from inhaling foreign objects.

Breathing adjusts to feelings and situations. We hold our breath when we are tensed up, when we anticipate certain situations and have time to prepare ourselves for this, e.g. when building up our body tension, or before jumping into the water.

As toddlers have very different experiences with water, it is necessary for the course instructor to deal with each child personally beforehand, so as to find out how they react from a reflexive, anticipative and emotional aspect, i.e. how each child copes with water.

The water-pouring method has proven itself for finding this out.

The *water-pouring* test should not be carried out until the child has gotten used to his water surroundings and is alert, attentive and able to take new things in.

Procedure of the water-pouring method

◆ The parents hold the child in the basket grip.

◆ The instructor is standing beside the parent, talks to the child, and tests his attentiveness by tapping a bowl on the water surface.

◆ If the child outstretches his hand, the instructor then fills up the bowl with water, and then pours it over the child's hand, arm, shoulder, back of his head up to the top, so that water pours over his face.

◆ If the child turns around towards the bowl again, is relaxed and shows signs of being emotionally contented, the procedure is repeated.

◆ During the second pour, the water should run over his face for about two seconds. When his eyes close and open (lid closure), his mouth makes chewing actions in order to relieve the tension in the facial muscles, he turns toward the bowl again, there are no signs evident of fear and discomfort in his facial expression, and his breathing has not stopped (feel the thorax), the child has then shown a positive or neutral (according to his facial and physical) reaction.

◆ In the case of a positive or neutral pouring test reaction, the child can be systematically introduced to brief diving situations.

◆ The pouring test reaction indicates the toddler's willingness to dive. Due to the changes in his day-to-day form, his current phase of development, his level of excitement and his willingness to take in new things, the test should be carried out in every lesson, in various forms. The exercises for diving are always prepared using a water tunnel, a hose, a watering can or other squirting games. They help to decide what kind of form the child is in, and if he is willing to dive.

◆ Further decisive criteria for the course instructor are the parents' body language and confidence in handling. It may be necessary to assess their behavior.

A distinguishing feature of this method is that it finds out the child's emotional willingness to dive on the one hand, and enables intervention

when the child is afraid of the water, on the other (desensitising). One can vary the test in its application (much/little water). It is important to point out that the water-pouring test is not necessarily combined with diving.

The child experiences the water, is able to adapt to it, and learns to protect himself (no swallowing of water or it going down the wrong way). Without any pressure or persuasion, it is even possible for a child to lose any fear he may have of the water by actively taking in the systematic procedure (perceptive learning). He can prepare himself for it by seeing, feeling, touching and sensing the water, and has time after the water-pouring test to classify, process and express this experience from an emotional and motivational aspect.

The parents and instructors can *read* from a child's behavior on a particular day whether the child accepts water in general, as well as diving. As the child's speech comprehension improves with age, it becomes easier to verbally discuss the procedures.

The water-pouring method in its five-phase procedure:

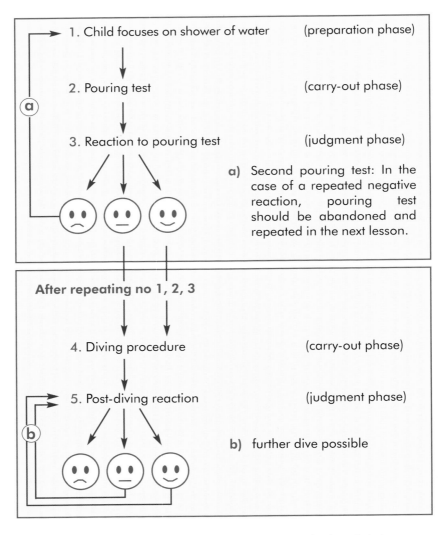

1. Child focuses on shower of water   (preparation phase)

2. Pouring test   (carry-out phase)

3. Reaction to pouring test   (judgment phase)

a) Second pouring test: In the case of a repeated negative reaction, pouring test should be abandoned and repeated in the next lesson.

After repeating no 1, 2, 3

4. Diving procedure   (carry-out phase)

5. Post-diving reaction   (judgment phase)

b) further dive possible

Fig 19: Course of procedure for water-pouring method and diving.

Only with successful test reactions does one receive sufficient information on a child's familiarity with the water and his willingness to dive. The child must be attentive with this new, oncoming experience. By no means may a child be surprised or suddenly confronted with it. He is prepared for diving by focusing on a person, object or place, and then diving towards this item of focus with his parent's help. The parents agree on this target on dry land *beforehand*, so as to support the child's strength of imagination.

In jumping, falling and sliding situations, as well as, in the airplane grip, the child has gradually gotten used to a splashing movement procedure with a dive to follow, and he now expects his head to go underwater. Going head-first underwater is a good idea as the water touches the child's hands and skull first before going into his eyes, nose and mouth. With this direction of movement and nose position, water generally does not enter the nose in the first place.

One second underwater is enough initially. The duration is increased only gradually, by e.g. letting the child come back up again after a jumping activity while keeping permanent eye contact with the child, and offering him a supportive hand when he needs it.

The above-mentioned fixed target that one agrees on beforehand is also important after diving, so that the child can orientate himself again. The more often the exercise is repeated, the more his self-confidence and feeling for safety grows.

Older children tend to learn to dive with the help of material (equipment), verbal, visually depicted or imitative (demonstration) commands. The edge of the pool or the pool steps can serve as a jumping platform. It is always helpful when the parents put aside their own shyness of going underwater, and demonstrate a dive (model).

The child is encouraged and motivated to dive in with them. From the third year of life onwards, the child even dives in by himself without any commands. He is then motivated enough to try it out himself.

A real test of strength begins with testing how long he can stay underwater, as well as the discovery that one can see underwater.

The following techniques and grips are suitable for various diving situations which are aimed at schooling the diving depth, distance or duration, but rather as a form of playful safety training:

◆ Diving in from a sideward swing:
The parents stand sideways in front of the edge of the pool, holding the child in the face-to-face grip. They pull their child sideways through the water towards the edge, so that his head, ear and face are touched by water (1). Following this outer swing comes a second inner swing which involves the eyes and corners of the mouth.(2)

The third swing starts off from above. The child touches the water with his hand and head, a wave rolls over his head. Having now been turned into prone position, the child comes back up again and is pushed toward the edge.

◆ Diving in after a drop from the armchair grip:
The parents stand in front of the edge of the pool, the child is sitting on their lower arm. By tapping on the water, the parents attract the child's attention to the water surface. Now they tell the child to jump towards the edge. With their free hand, they support their child under the chest when he comes up again, and glide him towards the edge. This exercise can also be carried out from the *shoulder seat or handbowl standing position*.

◆ Diving in from the airplane:

The parents stand in front of the edge of the pool holding their child in the *sandwich grip*, i.e. they support the child in prone position under his chest and hold him between the legs. The child is moved back and forth twice toward the edge of the pool, and then lifted up into the air. Staying in this position for a moment until the child has oriented himself to the water surface, he then dives out to the front, his hands stretch out automatically in front of his head (arms' supportive function).

When the child touches the surface first with his forehead, eyes and nose (nose dip), his attention is directed towards closing his eyes and mouth. It is only when the child has been frequently observed using these protective mechanisms that he is allowed to dive with his whole face, and later with his head.

If it does not work with the *sandwich grip,* one can also try using the *merry-go-round grip* where the child is grasped at his (outer) upper arm and (inner) thigh. The backward *trophy grip* can also be used.

◆ Diving in from a sitting position on the (high) edge of the pool:
The parents stand sideways in front of the pool wall, holding their child in the *sandwich grip*. The child throws a toy into the water in front of him, leans forward, and is then supported in his fall under the chest and at his back. He dives in head first, and comes back up again in front of the toy. This can also be done from the side of the pool with the child in sitting or standing position.

6.2.5 Ideas for Movement Using a Training Circuit

Doing activities at different stations is a creative and variable method of organization in a lesson. It fits in very well with a child's lively movement urge and intensive playing instincts, particularly in the second year of life, not neglecting to take his strongly fluctuating daily form, individual needs and different spans of attention into consideration. Station activites done with 2-3-year-olds can be used for practicing specific skills.

The toddlers can
◆ try out and get familiar with many pieces of game equipment
◆ choose how they want to play and practice
◆ work on different skills and gather experience
◆ try out the playing stations which vary in duration.

The number of different stations is to be selected in such a way that the children are busy with their parents without any waiting times even if they skip a station. Working with large pieces of equipment obviously takes up more time than with smaller items only, but this should not be a hindering reason. The size and form of the pool determine this factor. It is also possible to set up stations where the parents can demonstrate an exercise, and the children can copy it.

It is a good idea to use the corners of the pool for room orientation, and incorporate a changeover in activity emphasis.

Assuming the lesson takes place in a learner's pool (approx. 8-12m) with about 8 parent-child pairs, 4-6 stations are generally enough. Toddlers in their third year of life can also be offered help with their tasks in the form of picture materials (waterproof) which the instructor can hang up. The parents can look at the task beforehand, and then explain it to their child with language and in clear terms (learning by cognitive recording of language and pictures).

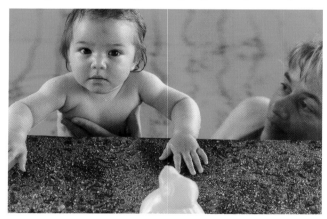

The exercises at the stations can be selected from the repertoire of exercise appropriate to age (see chapters 2.1 and 6.2.1).

The setting up of stations can either occur together with the group after the phases of familiarization and perception, or the course instructor can deliberately have it all set up before the lesson begins, so that the children can tear into the stations after the greeting phase. This positive aspect of wanting to experience the water is something which the instructor should make great use of.

Here are a few examples of movement ideas for station activities.

Theme: Making Music	
Station 1:	**Little bells**: These are hanging on a line.By swimming alongside them or touching them with hands or feet they can be made to ring.
Station 2:	**Rattles**: The rattles (shampoo bottles of various shapes and sizes, filled with peas, gravel etc.) are lying in the overflow drain. The children climb along the edge towards them, make noises with them, and take them out of the drain. After that they must throw the rattles back into the right place.
Station 3:	**Mat**: Drumming on the mat with a wooden spoon and small, upturned bowls. After that, drumming on the mat with hands and feet.
Station 4:	**Bottle bubbles**: Press empty bottles underwater, and let bubbles appear. The children dip their face in and blow bubbles in the water with their mouth.
Station 5:	**Metal spoons**: Swim from one side of the pool to the other and hit the bars of the ladder with spoons. The children climb out of the pool to do this, and when they have given back the spoon they jump back in to their parents.

Theme: Experiencing Water	
Station 1:	**Garden Hose**: A hose is placed on the tap/inflow so that the children are able to observe, and feel the flowing water which resembles a fountain.
Station 2:	**Water bowls**: The children transport water in bowls on a swimming board from one side of the pool to the other, lift the bowl, and then place it on the side. The children then climb off and jump to the board held by his parents.
Station 3:	**Water tunnel**: A perforated mat is lying at the edge. Water is poured over the tunnel when a parent-child pair pass by.
Station 4:	**Watering cans**: Water is gathered out of a container with a watering can, and poured into a pipe. Forward movement between two places.
Station 5:	**Mat with empty shampoo bottles**: The shampoo bottles are filled with water. By squirting water at each other, the children then squeeze and shake them out.
Station 6:	**Mirror (out of tin foil)**: Breathe out in water, observing this in the mirror, or spitting water against one's own reflection. For the older children, diving down and looking at oneself in the mirror.

Theme: Balls of fun

Station 1: the	Styrodur mats: This is lying, or is held at the edge of the pool. The children climb onto the edge of the pool, receive a ball from their parents, and let it roll along mat, sliding down afterwards. Finish up the slide with a dip or dive depending on ability.
Station 2:	Hoops: A hoop is lying on the water (held with a string and a 5kg diving ring). The ball should be pushed down under the water, the children blubber or dive inside. The parents can vary the degree of intensity by holding up the hoop—depending on ability. This exercise can be done backwards.
Station 3:	Tube: Place small balls within, a tube and pick them up at the other end.
Station 4:	Hoops: A hoop is held up over the water, or is hung up on a band. The children throw the ball through the hoop, fetch it, and throw it again.
Station 5:	Beach balls:The children lie down on their tummies on the slightly blown-up ball, and kick their way across to the other side of the pool.
Station 6:	Basket and bowling on a mat: The children have to hit the bowling pins (empty water bottles) with balls.

6.2.6   Perception Exercises

The ability to perceive with the senses and the body is something which can be developed and worked on in exercises.

The *optic area* deals with differentiating between colors and forms, and focusing on moving targets. Sounds and noises activate the acoustic apparatus.

Shapes, amounts, sizes and weights are recorded in the *tactile area* by the senses of touch. *Body orientation* is complex: the children become aware of various parts of the body by touching and naming them, and they build up their body scheme.

Orientation within a room does not only refer to the three-dimensional measurements, but also to the body itself within its limits, as well as the body position and balance. It is also possible to improve one's capacity of reaction and skillfulness in grasping, catching and throwing, and this work can be supported by acoustic or tactile signals.

6.2.6.1   Optical Area

The following game ideas are suitable for observing, looking for, and distinguishing according to color and shape:

◆ Setting the table: Place beakers, plates and spoons on a swimming board.

◆ Hiding game: One group hides objects under mats, boards and bowls; the other group has to find them.

◆ Four walls, four colors: Mark out each side of the pool with boards or cones. All objects lying in the water have to be gathered up and brought to the right area depending on their color.

◆ "Red, red, red is the colour of my clothes." When the color is mentioned in each verse then look for, grasp and hold up items of that particular color.

◆ Hiding game: All participants turn towards the edge of the pool. In the meantime, one parent-child pair hides under the mat tunnels or upturned paddling pools; the rest of the group look for them.
◆ "Hello, cuckoo" Each parent-child pair holds a swimming board in front of them. Every time they meet another pair they appear out from behind it and call out.
◆ "Sort out according to color" Hoops of different colors are floating around in the pool; the children have to place, e.g. building blocks of a particular color inside the right hoop.
◆ Balloons: Parents throw balloons up in the air, the children watch them as they fall down again, and try to catch them.
◆ Billiard table: Several parent-child pairs gather around a mat, tipping a ball to and fro and observing it.
◆ Ball game: Throw, kick (with the foot), push (with the hand), hit (with the head) a ball back and forth.

6.2.6.2   Acoustic Area

Sounds and noises are produced in the games that follow and serve to train the child's hearing.

◆ Drumming: With their hands, the parents and children drum on and under the water, on their mouth (Indian call), or on their stomach.
◆ Kicking orchestra: The course instructor (conductor) gets the children to kick around. On a certain signal the movements are stopped and

everyone listens to the quietness. Parents and children change over. Remember to vary volume levels (gradually kicking more gently/more intensively).

◆ Water story: The course instructor tells a story about the weather, or reads a poem:"It's drizzling, it's raining, it's pouring, it's hailing, thunder and lightning and back comes the sun." Children and parents make arm movements parallel to the story.

◆ Frog concert: The group begins to croak quietly, then gets louder, and thens stop abruptly following the course instructor's signal ("Pst!"). Hands and arms can make scooping movements, or the legs can do frog movements.

◆ Rattle song (one rattle per person): Rhythmic rattling to a song

◆ Rattle song (with two rattles): Rhythmic knocking with each other (e.g. "I've been working on the railroad").

◆ Blubber concert: In a frontal circle parents and children blubber bubbles into the water. They try to vary their tones in the process.

◆ Musical statues: The group moves through the pool to music. When the music stops, everyone stops, too, and listens to the sounds.

◆ Conductor: The group taps the water surface with their hands (loud/quiet) according to the conductor's signs and signals.

◆ Swans and ducks: Using pictures or commands, the instructor gets parents and children to carry out a swan's calm, gliding movements or a duck's noisy, flapping, quacking movements.

◆ Line tones: If the line is raised, the parents and children produce high tones with their mouth; when the line is lowered, the tones become deeper.

◆ Little dogs, big dogs: Using pictures or commands, the instructor gets parents and children to bark, to make dog-crawl movements with their arms, and move towards other parent-child pairs.

◆ "Clap handies, clap handies": The group forms a frontal circle. The children sit on their parent's raised thigh, facing outwards. They clap in time with the rhyme.

◆ Splashing circle with rhyme: Splash and paddle in rhythm with a verse.

◆ Bottle sounds: Blow into bottles, so that different sounds emerge.

◆ Blubber pipe: Blow through little pipes in the water to produce blubber sounds.

◆ Sound test: Using a wooden spoon, knock on different pieces of equipment at and around the edge of the pool, thus producing a variety of sounds.

6.2.6.3 Tactile Area

Game ideas for feeling and touching:

◆ "What's in the sack?": Feel three different objects through, e.g. a pillowcase, try and guess what they are, and then take them out.

◆ Cold, lukewarm, warm: Place bowls that are filled with water of different temperatures at the side of the pool, and let the children feel these differences.

◆ Soft and hard: Children feel the different textures of things by grasping sponges and pot scrubbers that are distributed in the pool.

◆ Round and pointy: Children take hold of and feel balls and cubes and then sort them out, e.g. on two separate mats.

◆ Light and heavy: Test the difference between the weight of empty bottles and those filled with water, and then sort them out onto two mats.

◆ Change in the ground surface: Let the children walk or crawl over the tiles, foam mats, artificial greens, etc

◆ Body wash: Parents and children wash each other with sponges, pot scrubbers and brushes, or say where they want to be scrubbed.

◆ Feel the wall and push oneself away from it: Push the children backwards in prone position towards the wall, let them touch this wall with their feet, and then get them to push themselves away again.

◆ Grasping with feet: Take hold of various toys that are lying in the pool by the feet, and transport them to the edge.

◆ Foot greeting: The children are held in the relax grip. Their parents push their child towards another pair of feet, and their feet say "hello." Variation: All the little feet say hello to each other in a circle, and then the parents lift up one of their own feet up to the surface.

◆ Foot catching: The parents are holding their child in the sandwich grip, and tell them to catch the other children's feet.

◆ Snapping hands: The parents are holding their child in the embrace grip, and they encourage him (by doing it first themselves) to snap hold of the other hands in the water, and say hello.

6.2.6.4   Body Orientation

Playing ideas for finding out one's body limits and body scheme:

◆ "Who is in the cave?": Place a parent-child pair under an upturned paddling pool. The other couples feel their heads, hands or body from ouside and from underneath.

◆ Body drawing: Place one's body, hand or foot onto a mat/ swimming board and then "draw" around it with the index finger.

◆ Hiding hands (song): "I'm looking for my fingers, please tell me where they are! Ah, they've come right back to me, tralalalalalala." Hands are hidden under a mat, and then revealed again. (Also suitable for other parts of the body.)

◆ Stuck under the bridge (song): "London Bridge is falling down, falling down etc." Wander through the bridge formed by two people's arms. One child is "caught," rocked, and then let by.

◆ Driving and tailgate: Run behind each other in a circle. One parent-child pair stops suddenly, the others drive into them.

◆ Up and over: Children move along the side of the pool hand over hand. The parents get into their way as obstacles and have to be climbed over.

◆ Covered with boards: Pull the child backwards through the pool in the relax grip, and cover him with swimming boards that are distributed around the pool.

◆ Collision: Holding the child in the trophy grip, push the children towards other children, so that their hands meet.

6.2.6.5   Spatial and Positional Orientation

Game ideas for perceiving one's own personal position and one's position within the room:

◆ "Puff, puff, puff, goes the big steam train, a tunnel's coming round the bend, I don't like driving on my own, so I take all my friends." (song): Cross under mats which form the tunnel.

◆ "All the children high in the sky": The children are held in the trophy grip and, after a signal, are pushed towards the edge, and then upwards, or pushed on mats and raised.

◆ "High and low, fast and slow, heavy and light, dark and bright": Parents hold their child in the face-to-face grip, and guide them into the various positions.

◆ "Back and forward, right and left, up and down , right and left." Children are held in the trophy grip within a circle and are moved according to the text.

◆ "We're wandering, we're wandering, from one place to the next and meet each other .....(in the circle) (verse): The group meets up in the circle, in the corner, in the tunnel etc.

Suitable balance exercises are:
◆ Jelly bellies: The children are sitting on a swimming mat: The parents shake the mat, and let it go again.

◆ "The big ship sails on the alley-alley-o....": The children are sitting on a mat and are pushed through the pool by their parents who make wave movements with the mat, thus causing water to splash over it.

◆ "Merry-go-round": The children are sitting on a mat. The parents turn the mat around and after each round there is a change in direction.

◆ Cat walk: Get the children to balance themselves across a "cat walk" of swimming mats, and then jump off at the end. It is also possible to extend this to an obstacle course.

◆ Taxi: The children are sitting on a board, and are pushed through the water by the parents. The children should decide the direction they are to drive in. Practice climbing on and off.

◆ Rodeo: The children are sitting on their parent's back. The parents challenge their child to hold on by riding in rodeo style.

6.2.6.6   Reaction Training

Game ideas for promoting reaction and hand skills

◆ Sleeping crocodile: The course instructor is a snoring crocodile in the middle of the pool. When he wakes up, he catches the children if they do not escape to the edge quickly enough.

◆ All change for heaven: When the music stops, the children have to swim to the edge as quickly as possible.

◆ Target throwing: The instructor pulls, e.g. a basin through the pool quickly. In the meantime, the children have to try and throw balls into the basin.

◆ Catch the ball: The instructor pulls a basin filled with balls through the water, the children are held in the trophy grip, and pushed or floated towards it quickly so as to get hold of a ball.

◆ Board swapping: On a signal, the children let go of their own boards, and look for another free board.

6.2.7   Playing with Materials and in a Group

Playing with materials and equipment plays a much more important role in toddler swimming than in baby swimming. The playing phases are significantly longer. The child plays more intensively, and with a higher level of concentration. The tasks become more and more adapted to the playing object. This form of play is a sign of physical and mental development progress.

In the second year of life, the child investigates, manipulates and, above all, tries out the various possibilities. Playing with children of the same age is not very fruitful, yet.

Because of his constantly expanding motor skills, the child is interested in everything within his reach, and he tests their function: flaps, drawers, cans and doors are opened and closed, bottles and water taps are twisted back and forth, bags and baskets are emptied and filled again. He begins to categorize, combine, and construct objects.

A toddler loves to repeat activities, and this is how he becomes more confident and skillful. He is positively motivated through his success with functions.

It is not until the third year of life that the child's social contacts are formed through communication and play; the child himself is searching for company. The child interacts with a playing partner or group and solutions are worked out; he observes and learns from others and is spurred on by happiness and physical involvement which in turn is favorable to his learning motivation and learning result.

Play situations cause the child to make comparisons which can trigger off feelings of aggression or fear.

The playing habits in the first and second years of life are characterized by *functional play*: the child plays with the body and parts of the body, carries out movements and deals quite roughly with objects and materials. He explores the close area first.

The older the child gets, the more mature he becomes for *construction games*, provided he understands the idea behind the activity; his playing behavior develops along with his spatial orientation: working on, shaping and creating with his hands, drawing, building and kneading.

The playing materials generally suitable for one- to three-year-olds are colorful building blocks of various shapes and sizes, boxes, cans, beakers, balls, rings, animals, cars and dolls. He is not interested in *fiction and role games* until the end of his third year, i.e. listening, observing, singing along, imitating persons and animals, stories and doll games.

The course instructor should include playing situations in his lessons in compliance with a clear concept: a *structured game* with ideas and suggestions, as well as a *creative game* which uses the participants' imagination, so as to moderate and create a new game idea together, or alternatively, a *free playing period* without guidance.

The number of playing materials used depends on the *children's stage of development*. One must take the health factor into consideration. The objects used should be *practicable* for use in water (i.e. washable and durable) and, from an educational aspect, should be *variable in use*, i.e. simple enough to arouse imagination and enhance the child's urge for versatile activity and movement.

The pool should be arranged into different areas: suction cups, plastic ropes, mats and plastic bands can be used as visual orientation guides for small groups, games or circuit activities.

Important for play is that both children and parents intensively get involved with an activity or person; this is what makes the game attractive, after all.
    The course instructor keeps an eye on and controls the *dosage level*, i.e. a suggestion is made and put into practice, a game is extended or shortened, the play stimulus is strengthened or broken down.

Toddlers move around searchingly in an *emotional swing* between curiosity and protection. When jumping and rollicking around, it becomes clear that being thrown up in the air or the "*Phew! Just barely caught*" feeling is only experienced as being positive when the child's own limits are not exceeded.
    Breaks are necessary when taking the child's performance limit into consideration.

Abrupt and sudden factors sharpen a child's perceptive abilities, and trigger off the impulse to react.

A word of warning here, however: even well-meant frights must have their limits. This holds for both the beginning and the end. So as not to disappoint the child, one systematically prepares him for the end of the game (announce: "So, three more times and then that's it."), and he can vent his emotions up to this point.

Below are some suggestions for play with a wide selection of different materials, so as to activate the children mentally, as well as in motor activity, balance and social behavior:

◆ Content games: Emptying and filling baskets, filling basins using bowls, and emptying them again.

◆ Transport games: Bringing and collecting building blocks to a mat; piling boards on a swimming mat and taking them down again, gathering up equipment.

◆ Seeking games: Looking for materials, (e.g. ropes) in a game with one or more parent-child pairs, and then getting hold of them.

◆ Building games: Placing beakers over each other, putting tennis rings onto a rod or the course instructor's arm, tying balls on a line or gathering balls in a pipe, building towers (vertical) with bricks, placing pull buoys or swimming mats over each other.

◆ Hiding games: Hiding objects or persons behind mats, under upturned paddling pools, or behind a line of cloths, and then looking for them,.

◆ Games in a circle: Picking up pieces, passing/pushing them on as well as throwing things away or to a person. The children are passed round in a circle.

◆ Group and contact games: Touching each other ("All in a muddle," narrow circle), pushing one another, (e.g. train), carrying, taking one another's hand, hanging on the other person's shoulder.

◆ Water games: Splashing, scooping, dripping, frothing up water, transferring it to other vessels. Producing waves, current, whirlpool.

◆ Functional games: Stirring with a soup spoon (cooking soup), cleaning the side of the pool with sponges. Hammering with a cooking spoon, opening cans, filling with water, closing cans and placing them into the cupboard (side of the pool).

◆ Finger games: Counting rhymes, verses and songs using hands and feet, speaking and singing fingers and toes, always including the child completely here.

◆ Sorting games: Distinguishing and categorizing objects according to color, shape and size (after two-and-a-half years to amounts, as well). Shape and jigsaw activities, recognizing pictures.

◆ Construction games: Placing puzzle pieces beside each other, setting building bricks beside and over each other (vertical and horizontal).

◆ Symbolic games: Swimming animals drink water and dive, dolls jump in from the edge of the pool.

Popular running games in the room are:

◆ Save yourselves..... (in your house): When the course instructor starts splashing with water, all participants look for protection under the swimming mats which have been placed on the side.

◆ Save yourselves.....(on an island): When the course instructor goes underwater as a crocodile all the children look for protection on a mat.

◆ Weather games: It's drizzling (participants let the water drip from their fingers); it's raining (participants throw the water into the air); it's stormy (the children froth up the water with their arms and hands or the parents pull them through the water to the left and the right); there's lightning (everyone gets out of the water and sits on the edge), and then the sun comes back up again (all jump back into the water again).

◆ Four walls, four colors: Each side of the pool is marked with an object or traffic cone of a particular color. The course instructor begins a rhyme: "Let's go for a walk, and go for a stroll, and then meet again at the *red* wall."

◆ Motor on, motor off: The children are in piggy-back position on their parent's back. The motor on and motor off positions are depicted in movement by the children kicking their legs, and the parents moving forward or coming to a halt. This game can also be used in the same way for stimulating arm movement. The children are then held in the trophy grip, and have to dig or paddle with their arms.

Playing with balls in the group:

◆ Keeping the field empty: Two groups throw or push balls out of their own field into the other field. This can also be varied to a ball-above-the-line game.

◆ Filling and emptying eggcups: One group places the distributed balls into empty bowls that are on boards or on the edge. The other group empties the bowls.

◆ Pass it on: A ball is passed on in a circle to the right, and after a signal it stops and changes direction again, accompanied by a verse ("This way, this way, stop and now the other way").

◆ All out: Any balls in the pool are thrown out to the side. Once all the balls are outside the pool the children are told to climb out, and throw them back in again.

◆ Chain transport: The balls are taken out of a large basin on one side of the pool and passed on in a row to a second basin on the other side.

6.2.8   Rituals and Songs

Greeting

"We're standing together, we're waiting to start, let's look all around first to see who takes part:
x-x is here, and x-x is here etc. etc...So now we can start*

Hello children , hello children, we're waving to you, hello children hello, children, first me and then you,
x-x is here, and x-x is here, hurra, we're all here, let's give a big cheer," (vary this with splashing, kicking etc. instead of waving).

"Look around and say hello, then we can begin.
We begin to dance and dance, we're da-anc-ing."

"Come over here, yes come to me, we want to swim,so come to me
I'm calling ....x-x : Yes, I am here
Come over here, we're swimming here." (Replace swim with jump, hop, kick etc).

"Hello, hello, come straight over here, and let us start singing and dancing and swimming,
hello, hello, come straight over here."

Getting used to the room and stimulating circulation

"Puff, puff, puff goes the big steam train, a tunnel's round the bend, I don't like driving on my own so I take all my friends."

"A teeny weeny water man is swimming round the pool,
he splashes here and splashes there, keeping nice and cool,
he swims through the water up and down, now he is turning right around."

"We're riding on the water train, water train, water train,
we're riding on the water train, we're all riding along.
We're stopping off at HOPtown, Hoptown, Hoptown,
we're stopping off at Hoptown, we're all hopping along.
(Movement: replace hop with jump, turn etc).

"We're wandering, we're wandering, from one place to the next, and meet up at the (circle)..."
or "We're wandering and wandering from one place to the other and we're meeting one another."

"We're splashing water all around, not so loud, without a sound, this is how we like to splash, splash all around." (Movement: replace splashing with hopping, clapping, kicking).

"All my little children, swimming round and round, kicking with their little legs, making quite a sound."

"The car goes brumm, the car goes brumm, starting slow, then off it goes, the car goes brumm, brumm, brumm."

"We're rocking here and swaying there, then we fly up in the air."

"Two little dicky-birds sitting on a wall, one named Peter, one named Paul, fly away Peter, fly away Paul, come back Peter, come back Paul." (Movement: with each foot)

Getting used to water—letting the body feel water— preparation for diving

"I'm looking for my eyes, please tell me where they are, ah they've come right back again, tralalalalalala." (Movement: replace eyes with other parts of the body).

"We're splashing, we're splashing, splashing all around, when my hands are feeling weak, then it's time to use my feet, we're splashing, we're splashing, splashing all around."

"All my little children are getting wet today, getting wet today, splishy, splashy, splishy, splashy, hip hooray!"

"It's drizzling, it's raining, it's pouring, it's stormy, it's loud, the sun it starts shining, way over the clouds." (Movement: hitting the arms on the water to describe the weather),

"We need our hands for splashing, splash, splash, splash"

(Replace with feet/kicking).
"Neptune calls all frogs: 'Ribbit, ribbit.'"
(Movement: parents jump with their child.)
or
"Neptune calls all blubber fish: 'Blubb, blubb.'"
(Movement: parents and children exhale at the water surface.)
or
"Neptune calls all dolphins: 'whooh, whooh.'"
(Movement: children glide through the water, held by their parents.)
or
"Neptune calls all diving birds: 'Dip, dip.'"
(Movement: parents and children dive.)

Gymnastics

"Move yourself, move yourself, bit by bit
move yourself, move yourself,that's how you keep fit,
move your arms, legs, shoulders, tummy and back
move yourself forward and back."

"O'Grady says......"

"Mr. Mince and Mr. Mance, they went for a dance,
they danced to the left , then danced to the right,
then danced like this, and kicked with bliss." (Movement: Guide
the legs, then bend, stretch and kick.)

"Horsey, horsey, don't you stop,
just let your feet go clippety clop,
let your tail go swish and your wheels go round,
giddy-up we're homeward bound."

Finishing off the lesson and saying goodbye

"Puff, puff, puff goes the big steam train,
it's time for x-x to go home,
he doesn't like it on his own,
so he's taking x-x along."

"We tap upon the water, before it's time to go,
we say goodbye, we say goodbye, waving to and fro."

"Little mouse and great big bear
rocking here and swaying there."

"Silently, silently is how the cat creeps
Silently, silently, look how she creeps,
along comes a little mouse, and all the cats cry out:
'Meooowww'."

"There once was a man who had a dog,
Bin-go, Bin-go, Bingo was his name,
B-i-n-g-o." (Movement: push the children into the middle of the
circle first, and then move away from each other. Or: the
children are held in a circle, and then pushed towards each
other.)

"When the moon is in the sky,
and the sun has said goodbye,
we are finished here today,
here's a kiss for on your way. (Movement: course instructor
blows a kiss into the group.)

"Red rover, red rover,
our swimming is over,
let's tidy the toys,
without any noise,
red rover, red rover,
our swimming is over."

6.2.9   Ways of Relaxing in the Water

"Rest is the natural mood of a well-regulated heart
that is at one with itself"
(WILHELM VON HUMBOLDT)

After hard work, the body demands a break for a long or short period, as well as to be able to relax after mental tiredness. The rule is to process what one has learned and, after letting off steam, to allow contentedness to set in.

Finishing off the relaxation phase with a certain ritual is generally perceived to be pleasant. Body, mind and soul can come to rest in harmonious surroundings and all those involved (course instructor, parents and children) can "refuel" again inside.

As children generally follow what their "trust persons" do, it is important that the adults—even for themselves—carry out this ritual as well, step for step, so as to avail of its relaxing effect. Learning how to relax is not child's play, but can nevertheless be practiced in a playful way.

When the necessary general conditions are fulfilled (no noise, no disturbances outside the pool, a pleasant water temperature, perhaps dimmed light), the instructor can begin with this last phase.

He starts introducing attentiveness and calm into the group in a narrow circle (*rest introductory phase*). He then describes the position for the parents and children.

One generally assumes the *relax grip* or *arm cradle* positions (with support at the back of the knees), or parents and children lie on mats or pool noodles.

One should set 5-10 minutes for this phase as the body cools out very quickly in water after all the activities.

Breathing becomes calmer, body tension should be dispelled down by associating one's own personal picture of this (*relaxation phase*) which allows warmth, heaviness, calmness, safety, familiarity, as well as contentedness to set in, similar to when lying tucked in and undisturbed in a soft bed or on warm sand.

Dimming the lights or closing one's eyes blocks out the visual stimuli of the surroundings, and helps one concentrate on one's own body.

As well as imaginary pictures, a relaxing effect can also be achieved through calm words ("You are lying quietly, calmly") or conscious tensing and loosening exercises for muscle groups or body regions (progressive muscular relaxation).

After the relaxation phase, the course instructor should take back activity again, bring the participants' body and mind back into real surroundings, as well as activate their circulation with certain exercises (*taking back phase*).

Stretching oneself, yawning, pulling faces, shaking and massaging parts of the body all help to react the body, so that pulse and breathing rates, as well as blood pressure go back to normal.

The lesson deliberately comes to an end without any follow-up turbulence, so that the child is able to fall asleep after all the intensive movement.

It sometimes happens that a parent-child pair is not capable of finding the necessary level of calm. Calming down is not a process that one can force; it also depends a lot on the child's form on that particular day.

In such a case, they should be offered an alternative playing opportunity slightly aside from the rest of the group, so as not to affect the overall harmony.

The instructor requires a good situative feeling when selecting the right methods here.

Examples of playful relaxation exercises for toddler swimming are:

◆ Relaxing to candlelight in a circle (in translucent colored beakers):

- Verse: *This candle moves around,*
  close your eyes and close your mouth,
  nice and tired, come to rest
  your body sleeping on my chest
  (Frontal circle, relax grip, sitting position, parents swing
  their child's body to and fro).

◆ Relaxing with physical tension:

- Contrast exercise: loud and quiet (kicking and silence)
- Progressive muscular relaxation: broomstick and rubber doll (stiff and loose).
- Storm and calm sea (hands digging in/ stroking the water).

◆ Relaxing to music:

- Music in breathing rhythm (60 beats per minute).
- Music is turned down, goes off.

◆ Relaxing with massage:

- Stroking (moving the flat hand over the body from the abdomen, back, legs and arms towards the heart).
- Shaking (the tissue is loosened up for a few seconds with rolling and vibrating movements).
- Circling (large and small circular strokes with one or two hands).
- Weather massage (the hands use different intensities of touch and depict sun, rain, hail and wind).
- Massage equipment (feet can not only be massaged with the thumb, but also with a "Footsie Roller" or massage ball).

◆ Relaxing with stories, pictures, animal imitations:

- Play a doll story ("The little, tired bear is looking for his cave").
- Tell a movement story (go from active to passive movements).

◆ Relaxing through rocking and swaying:

- Verse: *As I close my eyes to sleep,*
  not a sound, not a peep,
  my arms and legs are loose and free
  and the water carries me.

◆ Relaxing through breathing:

- Locomotive—breathing out loudly like an engine; breathing in deeply.
- Parents lay their child onto their chest, and breathe in and out with their chest visibly rising and falling.
- Parents breathe out deeply on their child's skin.

◆ Calming exercises with sounds

- Water sounds (rain drops).
- Rhymes: "Quiet, quiet, quiet" "Whisper, whisper, whisper."

6.3   Swimming and Buoyancy Aids

The theme *swimming aids* becomes an issue in parent-child courses in the second and third years of life. Firstly, the parents must be informed of the advantages and disadvantages of swimming aids and their use before getting to know about their range, type, and price.

One distinguishes between *swimming aids,* an apparatus that is attached to the child's body like swimming wings, and *buoyancy aids*, a swimming apparatus which the child can hold on to or lie on (a swimming board), so as to stabilize and support his position at the water surface. It is imperative that I emphasize that both aids do not guarantee a child's safety in the water.

The parents *must* constantly observe and supervize their child (cf. chapter 1.3). Later, when the child has much more strength in his legs, one can make use of *movement aids* (e.g. swimming fins), which enable and motivate the child to move around further and more quickly. The foot movements (instep stroke, kicking) are carried out more accurately.

The following swimming aids are generally available:
◆ Blow-up: Swimming wings, swimming cuffs, swimming discs with air chambers or styrofoam inside or else out of other foam variations (e.g *Swim fix, tadpole, dolphin discs*).
◆ Swimming rings in round, oval or horseshoe shape in various sizes; models with side support, chin rest, straps or seats (e.g. *swimstar, swimtrainer*).
◆ Swimming jackets or suits with various extras, e.g. with or without collar, with or without leg belt, with blow-up back and abdomen cushions or removable foam elements that have been attached to the jacket material.
◆ Swimming egg or swimming frame made out of plastic or some type of foam with a fabric belt.
◆ Swimming belts or corks made of plastic, cork or foam which are tied on with a fabric belt.
◆ Swimming cushions made of linen fabric with adaptable ties and fasteners for around the chest. The cushions then lie backwards at the shoulder blades.

The manufacturers label their articles with a recommended age group. This often specifies a maximum rather than minimum age.

The child's body weight, however, is the more significant decisive factor as opposed to his motor and coordination skills.

Type of Equipment

Swimming wing or cuffs

Swimming ring

Swimming jacket or suit

Swimming egg or frame

Swimming belt or cork

Swimming cushions

Specific article description	Starting age recommended by manufacturer
Swimfix	From 1-4 years
Swimming cuffs	None given
Swimming discs (dolphin)	Up to 12 years
Swimming wings	Up to 18 months
Open ring	Up to 4 years
Oval ring with side support and	Up to 1 year
chin rest	Up to 6 years
Horsehoe ring with straps (swimstar)	3 months-4 years
Ring with inner jacket	3 months-4 years
(Swimming trainer)	
Ring with baby seat (Babysitter)	3 months-4 years
Jacket with/without collar and leg belt	3-4 years
Suit with blow-up abdomen and	2-4 years
back cushions (Floaties)	
Swimsuit with pockets	2-4 years
for foam buoyancy aids	
Plastic frames with two air-filled buoyancy elements or fabric belt with an air-filled buoyancy element	2.5-4 years
Cork or foam blocks or plastic blocks filled with air are thread onto a rope or fabric belt. The number of blocks can be reduced.	2.5-4 years
Two linen cushions whose fibers expand in the water are blown up and are tied around the chest as a belt (Schlori)	2.5-4 years

Starting off with the primary aim of serving to promote movement, and the intensive interaction between parent and child, using swimming aids from the very beginning would ruin this aim of swimming immediately. For this reason, swimming aids should only be used from the moment when the child can support himself at the earliest (at approx. ten months, when he starts crawling). Even then, they are always to be used for a short period only so that parents and children do not get used to them.

We have to remember that swimming aids prevent children and parents from *naturally* coping with water. Swimming aids give a false sense of security and skill which toddlers are actually not capable of: the parents wrongly believe their child is in safety, they move away somewhat, and observe their child only sporadically. Or, the children move away from their parents as they believe that they are able to swim by themselves.

One is strongly tempted to disregard the importance of mutual dependence, the necessity of signal communication, as well as the feeling of trust in the other person. The technical aids are thus not a parental replacement, but merely have a supportive function.

They give both parents and children a certain freedom in movement, in not having to carry or hold on. By gradually reducing the buoyancy level, they can support the individual learning process. The question is whether a child experiences, in an appropriate way, how he can improve his abilities, and learn to trust the water's carrying force.

Parental body contact is combined under realistic conditions (i.e without external aids) with the learning phase for a particular age; the child's position in the water is not altered here, and the parents offer flexible and variable help. The parents themselves learn in the course where and how they can best support their child.

From practical experience, it is clear to see how suitable handling can skillfully adapt to the water surface, strength and body position; it does not restrict the child's freedom of movement, but rather enables grip and crossover movements, and these are decisive factors for the healthy development of a child's coordination of movement.

Moving around independently, and choosing the direction and position himself, is something that the child experiences only for a moment initially, and then gradually more and more.

Buoyancy aids are not only important for supporting the learning process; they also arouse the child's interest due to their floating ability. They support the non-swimming child in his effort to assume a swimming position at the water surface, and help to bring variety into games and exercises.

In a swimming lesson, it is possible to use the following:
◆ swimming boards or animals in the form of a board,
◆ swimming mats as rafts and running bridges,
◆ swimming bars,
◆ swimming lines, buoys or *tree trunks*,
◆ pull boys or swimming dumbbells,
◆ pool noodles with combining elements.

Other blow-up or plastic pieces of equipment can also be used as long as they enable the child to hold on or support his body. Before choosing such articles, one must ensure that they are suitable for the children's hands and body size, their body weight, and motor coordination skills.

As children often hold on to such aids for only a short time and lose their balance easily (tilt over), which is what stimulates play in the first place, the course instructor must organize and explain the run of events in the exercise beforehand (e.g. the movement direction), how the children are to be held, and who should help out.

IV APPENDIX

Alphabetical Index

Accidents, drowning 17, 82
Appropriate age to begin 10
Associative phase. 66
Automation 44

Basic motor skills . . . . . . .23pp.
Bathing . . . . .19p., 73pp.
Bicycle tube 77
Body perception 147
Body proportions . . .23, 147, 31
Body scheme 23, 31, 147
Buoyancy aids . . . . .175pp.

Care duties. 81
Circuit exercises . . .101, 141pp.
Closing of eyelids. 134, 135
Closing of mouth. 133
Cognitive phase 142
Coordination, eye-hand 46
Coordination,
    gross, fine, finest 46
Coordination, hand-foot 46
Course instructor 53pp., 81
Course planning . . .71pp., 89pp.

Defiant phase 10, 35
Development, physical 15
Development, motor . . . . .15pp.
Diving . . . . .133pp.

Early swimming badge 9
Ears 46
Epiglottal cramp 85

Fear of depth 10
Fear of separation 10, 35
First aid . . . . .81pp.
Far senses 32
Functional play 96, 155

Games 66pp., 78,
    87pp., 91pp., 111pp.
Getting changed 79
Grip ABC . . . .64, 66pp., 111pp.
Group size 71, 142
Gymnastic exercises 107

Hyperactivity 45, 46

Imitation 37
Injuries caused by falls . . .82, 83
Integral motivation 89, 90

Language development 36
Learning . . .7, 65pp., 72, 135, 142
Learning movement 62
Lesson structure . . . . .93pp.
Lesson unit . . . . . .10, 72, 93pp.

Method of self-rescue 17
Methodical principles 54
Minimal cerebral dysfunction. .47
Model effects 51
Movement aids . . . . .175pp.
Movement repertoire . . .24, 142
Muscular tension, hypertonic .45
Muscular tension, hypotonic . .46

Near senses 32
Noticeable movement
    defects . . . . .43pp.

Toddler Swimming

Object Permanence 31

Parental role . . . . .49pp.
Perception, acoustic 33, 148
Perception development . . .31pp.
Perception disturbances . . .43pp.
Perception exercises . . . . .147pp.
Perception, optical 147
Perception, tactile 150
Poisoning 82, 83
Pulse 86

Relaxation . . . . .101pp.
Relaxation exercises . . . . .103pp.
Rescue abilities 82
Role model 31, 38

Safety behavior 17, 84
Safety training 17, 19, 138
Sensory-motor integration . . . 28
Stimulus 31, 65, 66
Strengthening exercises 107
Swimming abilities . . .40pp., 67, 92, 103
Swimming aids . . .84, 103, 175
Swimming behavior . . . . . .62pp.
Swimming, definition 9
Swimming exercises 62
Swimming rules . .21, 73, 77, 81
Swimming technique 67

Tactile oversensitivity 47
Toilet training 40pp., 73

Water accustomization . .58, 89, 133pp.
Water, coping with 103
Water, depth of 82
Water intoxication 20, 49
Water phobia 20
Water pouring test 93, 133
Water properties 13
Water temperature 20, 44

Photo & Ilustration Credits

Photo Credits:

All photos including the cover photo are by Mathilde Kohl except for the photos on page 75 (Colettei), pp. 16, 26, 27 (Ahrendt), p.37 (Schmidt).

Illustrations:

Markus Linden & Ulrike Bakiakas

Cover Design:

Jens Vogelsang

Contact:

Dr. Lilli Ahrendt
Kieselstr. 5
40235 Düsseldorf
Germany
+ 49 - 211 - 9890727

Lilli Ahrendt

Baby Swimming

A specifically developed teaching concept, the Grip ABC, the "water-pouring" diving method and numerous ideas for movement and games are all presented here.

Who can take part in baby swimming, how this course is run and what you have to consider when being in the water with a baby is dealt with, as well as the critical discussion of the question why a child's development can be stimulated in water, and why this element water can rouse our bodies and senses in such a special way.

200 pages, full-color print
Numerous photos, 27 illustrations
Paperback, $5^{3}/4$" x $8^{1}/4$"
ISBN 1-84126-077-0
£ 12.95 UK / $ 17.95 US
$ 25.95 CDN / € 16.90

Anz Toddler Swimming

MEYER
& MEYER
SPORT

MEYER & MEYER Sport | sales@m-m-sports.com | www.m-m-sports.com